Other Temptations of Jesus

Other Temptations of Jesus

Lenten Studies for Adventurous Christians

JOHN HENSON

Foreword by Rowan Williams, Archbishop of Canterbury

John Hunt
Publishing Limited

Copyright © 2004 John Hunt Publishing Ltd
46A West Street, Alresford, Hants SO24 9AU, U.K.
Tel: +44 (0) 1962 736880 Fax: +44 (0) 1962 736881
E-mail: office@johnhunt-publishing.com
www.johnhunt-publishing.com
www.0-books.net

Text: © 2004 John Henson
Design: Nautilus Design

ISBN 1 84298 140 4

A CIP catalogue record for this book is available from the British Library.

Printed in England by Ashford Colour Press Ltd, Gosport, Hants.

TABLE OF CONTENTS

FOREWORD

What would Christianity look like, what would Christian language sound like, if we really tried to screen out the stale, the technical, the unconsciously exclusive words and policies, and to hear as if for the first time what the Christian Scriptures were saying? John Henson has devoted much of his life to wrestling with this challenge, and has for many people made those Scriptures speak as never before – indeed, as for the first time. Patiently and boldly, he has teased out implications, gone back to roots, linguistic and theological, and re-imagined the process in which a genuinely new language was brought to birth by those who had listened to Jesus because they knew they were in a genuinely new world.

Some of John's versions will startle; but only because we have forgotten what the impact might have been in the ancient world of a small library of books written in the dialect of the streets and shops, with many of the leading characters identified by slightly outlandish nicknames. And also, because we have not much living language left for authority figures, we fail to sense the impact of the images of royalty and so on in the pages of Scripture; we need other terms to make them come alive.

John's presentation of the Christian gospel is of extraordinary power simply because it is so close to the prose and poetry of ordinary life. Instead of being taken into a specialised religious frame of reference – as happens even with the most conscientious of formal modern translations – and being given a gospel addressed to specialised concerns – as happens with even the most careful of modern 'devotional' books – we have here a vehicle for thinking and worshipping that is fully earthed, recognisably about our humanity. Here are sensitive meditations, blunt and beautiful prayers, familiar hymns made fresh (polished and re-set as John likes to say). The Gospels tell us that Jesus' unprofessional and unreligious audiences heard him gladly: if they are to hear him gladly today, they will need something like John's renderings for this to be plausible. His work is for a large part of the 'religious' reading public a well-kept secret; I hope that this book will help the secret to be shared, and to spread in epidemic profusion through religious and irreligious alike.

Rowan Williams
Archbishop of Canterbury

PREFACE

This volume represents the first of a trilogy, but is being published second. The other parts of the trilogy are (2) *Other Communions of Jesus* (pub.1994) and (3) *Other Prayers of Jesus* (yet to be published). All three began as the substance of devotions on three consecutive Lents for the Anglican communion at Glyncoch. *Other Temptations* was also delivered at other Anglican churches in the Pontypridd neighbourhood.

As in *Other Communions* a scriptural study led to alternative insights into what is meant by the Lord's Supper, so *Other Temptations* leads by means of a similar study to an alternative understanding of the place of temptation in the Christian life.

The author wishes to thank the rank and file Christians who first inspired and heard these studies in whole or in part, especially the congregations of several churches in Pontypridd. He wishes to thank his own minister, Rev. Dr Mary Cotes, for her inspirational preaching and conduct of worship, which gave him the spiritual energies to carry on with the work, and Archbishop Rowan Williams for his support and encouragement.

This book is dedicated to Russell Howells, the

leading elder in his church for many years, and to his late wife Doreen who were together true and helpful friends to John and his family, as Russell continues to be. They will not mind their names being joined by that of Douglas Davies, John's friend and theirs, also for a long time a leading elder in the same church and a saint.

1
The Fourth Temptation

> After getting God's Spirit at the river Jordan, Jesus felt ready for the task ahead. But first he was moved to spend some time in the desert. This gave him the chance to get clear in his mind which direction his life should take. (Luke 4:1-2, *Good as New*)

> When the devil had finished every test, he departed from Jesus until an opportune time. (Luke 4:13, *NRSV*)

A few years ago I was sitting in a Cardiff pub, chatting to some friends over my drink of pineapple juice, being one of the dying breed of teetotallers. Two separate topics of conversation intertwined. One topic was our least favourite food. I had no difficulty in identifying my pet hate – cheese. I had been unable to eat it since my childhood days and the least suspicion of it in a dish would cause me to heave. The other topic was Lent and what each of us intended to give up. Some wag came up with a brilliant idea. Instead of giving up something we enjoyed doing, why not take up something we didn't enjoy. I could take up eating cheese! Before the night was out, without any alcohol to weaken my wits, I had vowed to have a go. I started with the tiniest bit of toasted mild cheddar and worked my way up. By the end of Lent I had learnt to nibble a variety of cheeses, including Stilton. Lasagne is now one of my favourite dishes. I don't know how I managed without it all those years. The following year I learnt how to eat beetroot and enjoy it. I was less successful the year after with onions. I now eat them, but they are not a favourite. The day I learn to eat a pickled onion I will have reached a rare peak of holiness! I soon ran out of new things to eat, though I have yet to sample raw oysters, caviar or paté de foie gras. Less frivolously, you may think, well beyond my fiftieth year, I used one Lent to take up cello lessons and achieved a grade 5 (not in one Lent!), and another Lent I commenced driving lessons and passed my test first time. Then my family suggested that if I really wished to impress I should take up something I really loathed – sport. Not only do I not enjoy sport, I help this aversion along with the conviction that sport was invented by the controlling classes to do away with play. Play is natural, spontaneous and therapeutic. Rules and competition are the death of play. I happen to believe that obsession with rugby football is the worst thing that ever happened to Wales. (At this point a proportion of my readers will wish to read no further!) However, I accepted my family's challenge and took up playing badminton with my son-in-law. I have found it enjoyable and healthy.

Instead of keeping score, we pay homage to the principle of Lewis Caroll, 'All have won, all must have prizes!'

I have discovered, in company with others, something very important about the Christian life. It is more a matter of what you do than what you don't do. It is not about 'giving up' but 'taking up'. I was brought up on a version of Christianity that seemed largely to do with a series of naughty musn'ts. Don't drink, don't gamble, don't swear, don't put the washing out on Sunday, don't even think about sex, etc. Some had a longer list than others. There *are* things a Christian should not do. A Christian should not judge others! But the call of Jesus to discipleship is based on two maxims, both positive – Love God and Love your neighbour. Anything we decide, as individuals, we should not do, whether in Lent or at any other time, should be based on that positive call, and not on pious ideas of holiness and self-sacrifice or the desire to be spiritually one up. There are too many miserable Christians and we have given the world the impression that religion is to do with being depressingly serious. Jesus said, 'I want you to have a life packed with good things' (John 10:10, *Good as New*). Even in Lent we should remember not only the Jesus who took up the cross, but the Jesus who supplied the wine at a wedding, who enjoyed parties and being invited out to lunch, who put up his feet in the home of Mary and Martha, and went for an

evening's cruise across the lake with his friends.
Jesus was accused by his enemies of over-eating and
drinking and of keeping company with extremely
unholy people. The great German theologian Karl
Barth said, 'Puritans should remember it is possible
to be a non-smoking, teetotal vegetarian, and still be
Adolf Hitler.'

The ministry of Jesus begins in Matthew and Luke
with the story of the temptations of Jesus in the
desert. How many temptations did these Gospel
writers record? At first glance there appear to be
three. We know them well. Turn stones into bread,
jump from the top of the temple, employ the enemy's
methods – bribe, show off, bully. We shall return in
the concluding chapter to the question of a personal
devil. Enough to say at this point, that the choices
facing Jesus were the same, whether it was some
malign spiritual being, or social pressures and
influences which beckoned him in the wrong
direction.

Luke hints at a fourth temptation. The devil
departed 'until an opportune time.' That is, the life
of Jesus would not be a constant, continual battle
with temptation. The experience of testing would
come and go. There were communities of monks in
the desert, the Essenes among them. Perhaps some of
these were the angels who looked after Jesus at the
end of his fast. They were people who had turned
their backs on the world and society in order to
spend their lives sharpening up their holiness. Their

life was, by choice, a non-stop struggle against temptation. The devil was always present, urging them to compromise their standards, to ease up on this or that ascetic exercise. They were convinced that they and they alone were God's true people, doing God's will. If Jesus had joined them we would never have heard of him!

The fourth temptation was the temptation to see the whole of life primarily as a battle against temptation. Jesus was being tempted to spend all his time playing the devil's game on the devil's terms. He would be so preoccupied with fighting sin as to have no energy left for any positive good, no time for life in all its fullness. Jesus resisted the temptation to waste his life playing a game of chess with the devil. He had better things to do!

It is because Jesus did not spend all his energy fighting temptation, that when genuine temptation came to him, he was able to withstand it. He did not look upon every invitation to a party or every encounter with a shady character, or every new thought and idea as bringing with it the possibility of sin. For the most part he was able to take a relaxed attitude to what other people regarded as the devil, so that when the devil really did speak to him, he was able to recognise that false note, the cunning line of argument. All he had to do was to remember the voice in the desert, the kind of propositions it made, and he was on his guard.

This series of studies takes a look at stories from

the Gospels that illustrate the way in which temptation came to Jesus during his ministry. They are occasions when 'the devil' found another 'opportune time'.

Lenten Hymn

Jesus, going without food,
In a rocky desert place,
Hot by day and cold by night,
Stared all evil in the face.
Hard it was for that young man,
With his famous appetite,
To forsake friends' company,
Swinging parties, laughter bright.

Scorpions sporting deadly tails,
Snakes in slithering twists and bends,
Lions and wolves with cruel fangs,
– Not the easiest of friends!
Great decisions to be made –
Power or service? Love or fame?
Flee the world or be its mate?
Lead revolt or heal the lame?

Who were those who came to care
For the Christ, exhausted, weak?
Lepers' commune? Desert friars?
They were angels, so to speak.
Praise to God; Give Jesus thanks

That he made the loving choice;
Sinners welcomed, fasts postponed,
Desert people find their voice.

(After 'Forty days and forty nights' G. H. Smyttan 1822-70. Best to tune 'Glad with Thee', Geoffrey Beaumont)

2
Save Me from my Friends

Mark 1:21-39 and Mark 5:1-20

> In the morning, before dawn, Jesus got up
> and went to a deserted spot to talk with
> God. Simon and his companions came
> looking for him. When they found him they
> said, 'Everyone's looking for you.' Jesus
> said, 'Let's go on to the other villages round
> about so I can share the Good News with
> them as well. That's what I'm here for!'
> (Mark 1:35-38, *Good as New*)

> As Jesus was getting into the boat, the man
> who had been cured begged to go with him.
> Jesus would not let him, but said, 'Go home
> to your own people and tell them what God
> has done for you and the kindness you've
> been shown.' He went around the whole
> area east of Lake Galilee telling what Jesus
> had done for him. And everyone was
> amazed. (Mark 5:18-20, *Good as New*)

Jesus moved from the desert to Nahum town
where he taught in the local place of worship and
helped a man who was suffering in his mind. Then

he went to enjoy hospitality in Rocky's home on the seafront and brought healing to Rocky's mother-in-law. At the end of the day there was an open-air meeting outside the front door and more people were healed and comforted. Temptation was left behind in the desert. 'The devil' and his murmurings were drowned out by the voice of human need. This was the life! This was the ministry to which Jesus had been called! This was positive! He was actively doing the will of the Loving God. But early next morning, Jesus was out in the lonely quiet place again, talking with that Loving God, thinking things through, planning strategy. 'Watch out Jesus, here it comes again!'

The friends of Jesus arrived, led by Rocky. They were wondering where Jesus had got to. 'Everyone's looking for you.' Jesus had become a star in Nahum town overnight. He had found a captive audience. This would be a great place for the guru to take his permanent seat. Surrounded by a supportive and appreciative fan club he could exercise a powerful ministry. People would travel for miles around to sit at the feet of 'Jesus of Capernaum'. But Jesus said, 'Let's go on to the other villages round about so I can share the Good News with them. That's what I'm here for!' Temptation dealt with for another day. Off to visit the other communities, including Nazareth, his hometown, where he was going to get a bumpy ride.

Jesus was tempted by his friends to settle in congenial surroundings and to ignore the call to move on. It was the temptation to a narrow area of experience and a limited clientele of people.

Where is our Nahum town? Where is the place we feel safe, comfortable and appreciated? The call away from Capernaum is the call away from our own preferred centre. To be truly ecumenical (= world-wide) means to associate with, to strive to understand and value, to accept as brothers and sisters, not only those who are nearest to us and most like us, or those with whom we would naturally be most at ease, but those who are least like us, who do things most differently, and who we find most difficult to get on with. Even when we have thus stretched ourselves to include all those who wear the Christian name tag (a daunting task), we must remember that the way of Jesus is out of the synagogue, out of the settled community, out of respectable society. There is no chance ever to settle down and be comfortable. There is no bolt hole from an uncongenial and hostile world. We must be ready to adventure with Jesus, to go somewhere new. That is the road to 'life in all its fullness'. Bye bye, Nahum town, welcome world!

Sometimes temptations can come to us in reverse or inside out. Jesus was never to allow himself to be tied down to a place or be identified with any centre. He was a New World traveller. He made return visits here and there and had friends, who made him welcome, in many useful stooping-off places. But he never stayed long enough to be identified with any one place. There is no Christian Mecca, despite the failed attempt of one Christian denomination to fix one. Jesus would not be stuck to Nahum town. But could Nahum town get stuck to him?

The journeys of Jesus frequently took him well into Gentile territory, an aspect of his ministry which until recently has been insufficiently taken account of. The Gentile mission began with Jesus, not with his reluctant followers. Even had Jesus wished to ignore the Gentiles, he could not have done so. The Roman world was cosmopolitan. All races mingled and mixed everywhere, except the inner courts of the Jewish Temple. But Gentiles could and did attend the synagogues and there were Gentiles in every crowd that followed Jesus. When Jesus visited Gentile territory the Gentiles probably outnumbered the Jews in his congregation. An examination of his contacts with the Gentiles is a subject for a separate study. Here we examine the case of one of them. The family of the 'Man of Gadara', as he is traditionally styled, lived in or near the town of Kursa, on the eastern shore of Lake Galilee, in what was then called 'The Region of the Ten Towns'. It was mainly Gentile territory. The presence of pigs as part of the local economy is a sure indication of this, as it was for the 'Prodigal' in the 'Far Country'. The man may have served in the Roman army and his rough experiences may have been responsible for his severe mental condition. His behavioural problems made him the terror of the community and a social outcast. Jesus cured him using a form of crisis therapy, pre-dating modern psychiatric techniques. Jesus convinced the man that his devils were running off with the pigs as Jesus drove them down the slope into the lake. The local farmers were not at all happy! Jesus was asked to leave the district, which he would have done in time anyway. The man volunteered to be a disciple. He was no more popular after his cure, it would seem, than before. He might relapse. A good idea, in everybody's interests, for Jesus to take him with him. Here comes the tempter – not in the pigs, but in a reasonable proposition.

Jesus was not an exorcist first and foremost, but a healer. He was man of his time and had to take the popular belief in evil spirits seriously. To what extent he shared this belief it is not possible to say with confidence. He used the language and pictures of his day. The healing of this Gentile from over the water is the most dramatic of his exorcisms, requiring the element of shock because of the severity of the case. Normally Jesus performed such cures with a brief word and total absence of the palaver in which other exorcists indulge, then and now. Because Jesus was a healer, he was more concerned about the real cause of the illness, hence his careful questioning of the man beforehand. He was also concerned about after-care and the man's relationships with his family and friends. It may be that difficulties within the family had contributed to the man's illness and desire to escape from reality. Jesus considered that the man must learn to integrate himself into his family and community if the cure were to be complete. There had been enough excitement in the army. Now was the time for rest and quiet and normality. Jesus could also do with a friend and representative in that district. In time the man would change the unfortunate impression the incident with the pigs had made on the locals and be an advertisement for the cause of Jesus and his New World.

The voice of the tempter argued otherwise. What a great disciple this man would make! The first Gentile on the team! He would owe everything to Jesus. Unlike the others, he would have given nothing up to follow him. He would be 100% loyal, hang on Jesus' every word, obey every instruction to the letter. He would get on well with Maggie (Mary of Magdala) who also had been cured of a bunch of devils and probably also with Larry, the beloved disciple, who had also emerged from a graveyard after a depressive illness. He would not make an empty boast like Rocky that he would go with Jesus to prison and to death. He would do so, gladly. He was not afraid of physical pain. He had a record of self-inflicted wounding. He would have proudly hung beside his leader on the cross and returned the taunts of the priests. Surely Jesus couldn't say no to a man like this? He could and did. Jesus had said goodbye to Nahum town. He didn't want Nahum town travelling around with him. He wanted followers and friends, not fans or sycophants. His fishermen, society ladies, terrorists, prostitutes, traitors, hotheads and doubters were a mixed and difficult bunch. They were not yes-persons. From them he would get awkward questions, heated debates, falling-out and making up again. The Complete Person ('Son of Man') wanted a lively think tank, not a selection of stooges. He wanted people he could consult and who would give him an independent judgement. Was he Messiah? How could he be sure? Ask the gang – they would give him an honest answer. Was his plan to make a stand in Jerusalem a wise one? Before embarking on it he discussed it with the troops. Jesus was at the opposite pole from the Hitlers and Stalins of this world who could not take criticism and ruthlessly repressed it. He enjoyed argument and repartee, treated his followers not as subordinates but as friends, responded positively to constructive criticism. The one who said, 'If you've got ears, use them!' practised what he preached. He knew how to listen. It was a high-risk strategy. His chosen friends would let him down. One would be marked out as a vile traitor to ease the consciences of the rest. But these were the people Jesus chose as his constant companions. The man from Kursa reminded Jesus too much of Nahum town. He wouldn't do at all.

Prayer

Friend Jesus, help us to know your companionship as
we try to spread your Good News.
We want to use your methods and share your motives.
We don't want to do anything for show;
we are not out to get a buzz;
we must be careful not to rob people of their freedom.

Save us from outdated ways of speech and patterns of
thought which
make the Good News sound like old news.
Save us from going on about sin instead of giving the
invitation to new life,
so turning the Good News into bad news.
Save us from narrow-mindedness,
which turns the Good News into good news for some
and not for others.

As we create a your new community of love, we aim
to do so without walls and without barriers.
Show us how false we are when we work for a unity
which depends on excluding others.
May your Spirit give us her gifts of imagination and
invention, sensitivity and daring.
Help us to realise that only when the Good News
becomes good news for the whole universe will it
become good news for us.

Amen.

3
Goodbye to the Old Testament

Luke 9:51-56 and Jeremiah 31:31-34

The life of Jesus was drawing to its climax. Jesus was determined to go to Jerusalem. He sent some of his friends on ahead of him to book accommodation in the places they were to pass through. They tried a village in Samaria but the people there showed their racial prejudice by having nothing to do with them. They realised Jesus was a Jew because he was on the way to a festival in Jerusalem. James and John were angry about this and said to Jesus, 'Leader, would you like us to ask God to send lightning from the sky to set the village on fire?' But Jesus gave them a stern talking to. He said, 'You must put a stop to those angry feelings of yours. The Complete Person doesn't set out to kill people but to bring them to life.' So they went on to the next village. (Luke 9:51-56, *Good as New*)

Jesus and his friends were in Elijah country. They

were in the region of Samaria. The town of Samaria had been the capital of Ahab, the king who introduced the worship of Baal under the influence of his foreign wife, Jezebel. Elijah the prophet challenged Ahab and condemned him for his disloyalty. It was on the nearby Mount Carmel that Elijah had settled the issue by calling down fire from heaven and ordering the mass slaughter of Baal's prophets.

Much water had flowed under the bridge in Samaria since Elijah's time. The northern tribes of Israel had been dispersed by the conquering Assyria, never to re-establish themselves. The later Samaria contained among its population fragments of the decimated Israelites and heathen elements intermingled with them. The result was a heretical and unorthodox version of the Jewish religion. The true-blue Jews of the remaining two tribes who returned from their exile in Babylon to re-found their capital Jerusalem would have nothing to do with this Samaritan hotchpotch, whose semi-heathen customs reminded them of the old Baal worship.

In the time of Jesus, Jews would normally avoid entering the territory of Samaria, and in order to go from Judea to Galilee would make a detour across the River Jordan. Jesus had no such qualms. His love stretched across the barriers of race and religion. He had a particular soft spot for those others despised. So he travelled from Galilee to

Jerusalem via Samaria.

The Jews did not like the Samaritans and the Samaritans returned the compliment. So when Jesus sought hospitality in a Samaritan village, sending his disciples to make the arrangements, the reaction of the locals was hostile. Here was a Jew – an orthodox Jew as far as they knew – on his way to Jerusalem for a Jewish festival, expecting hospitality from Samaritans who would not have been allowed past the Court of the Gentiles in the Temple, and probably would have been spat at there. Their answer was, 'You don't care for us, why should we care for you?'

Several temptations were possible at this point, including anger, frustration and incomprehension at the attitude of the Samaritans. James and John fell straight away. Jesus had a nickname for them, 'Boanerges', 'Thunder and Lightning'. They were known for their quick bad temper.

> 'Leader, would you like us to ask God to
> send lightning from the sky to set the village
> on fire?'

Although they were indulging in an outburst of bad temper, their thought processes were perfectly logical as good Jews of that time. This was Elijah country. The Samaritans, as ever, were apostates. As they spurned Elijah centuries before, now they were spurning the Messiah. God was a God of justice and judgement who vindicated his elect and put evildoers to shame. If Elijah could call down fire from heaven in the name of God, how much more God's Anointed?

This temptation came nowhere near the mind of Jesus and quickly he put Thunder and Lightning to rights.

> 'I'm not out to kill people, but to bring them to life.'

But there were possibly other, less extreme, temptations on the borders of Jesus' consciousness. The temptation, maybe, to go back on his attempt at racial inclusiveness, to regard people of other races and cultures as too much of a challenge, as liable to lead to complications and misunderstandings. Better, perhaps, in view of this experience, to stick to your own kind and leave others to find God in their own way. We know Jesus did not fall for this temptation. Quickly afterwards, according to Luke (chapter 10), Jesus recruited a team of an additional seventy or so workers whom he sent abroad into Gentile territory, even instructing them not to upset their hosts by insisting on kosher food. According to Mark and Matthew he conducted a communion service among the Syrians and Phoenicians in the north.

The temptation to give up on people who were unresponsive, whoever they might happen to be, was one Jesus had to face all the time. Here we find him

responding to rejection, not by losing heart, but by
having another go. Perhaps the approach to the
Samaritans had been too sudden for them to make a
positive response. Perhaps his friends had not been
sold on the idea, and in their approach to the
Samaritan villagers had sent out negative vibes.
Christians should never assume, when they feel
rejected, that the fault lies with those who do the
rejecting. It may be our fault for invading the space
of others without a by-your-leave, or it may be that
our agenda is all too obviously, 'We are the ones
who know what's what, and we are going to tell
you!' Jesus got it right by simply asking the
Samaritans for their help and putting himself at their
mercy or in their debt. Perhaps his friends were
embarrassed by such an admission of dependence,
and it showed.

A much more fundamental temptation underlines
this incident. Elijah is the key. Elijah represents the
religion of time past. Together with Moses he stands
as one of the twin pillars of the Old Testament.
James and John felt they were on such safe ground
in their request to Jesus to call down fire from
heaven. Next to Moses, there was no greater
authority in their religion as to what should be done.
But Jesus was the bringer of the New Testament,
which means that Moses and Elijah had had their
day. When Luke describes the 'transfiguration' of
Jesus on the mountain, just before the story of the
journey through Samaria (9:28), Jesus is pictured

with Moses and Elijah, or so the disciples take the shadowy figures to be. But then comes a voice from the sky, 'THIS is my Own, my Chosen; listen to HIM!'. Luke says, 'After the voice, they saw Jesus again, *but he was on his own.*' Jesus, as the bringer of the New Covenant, replaces Moses and Elijah as the one we are to listen to.

We need to revise our understanding of the expression 'New Testament' or 'New Covenant'. We use the words 'Old Testament' to describe part of our Bible, the part from Genesis to Malachi. This is a mistake. It's insulting to the people of the Jewish faith. It brands their scriptures as being out of date, which they are not and never will be. They are ever new and fresh for the Jewish people and should be new and fresh for us. These books should be introduced as 'The Hebrew Scriptures' and what we call the New Testament as 'Early Christian Scriptures'. The concept of the New Covenant occurs first of all, not in the Christian Gospels, but in the book of the prophet Jeremiah. The New Testament begins in what we call 'The Old Testament'. John the Dipper is found in the pages of the Gospels, but he is an Old Testament character, reminding people of Elijah. That's why Jesus says, 'I assure you that John the Baptist is greater than anyone who has ever lived. But the one who is least in the Kingdom of Heaven is greater than John' (Matthew 11:11, *GNB*).

The two religions, Old and New Testaments, are

scattered in Hebrew and Christian scriptures, often side by side and sometimes difficult to disentangle. How do we tell them apart? There are three areas of distinction: 1) The picture of God; 2) How we relate to God; and 3) How we regard one another, especially our enemies. There is also an Old Testament and a New Testament understanding of sex, but I shall deal with that big subject in another book.

THE PICTURE OF GOD

The Old Testament picture of God is based on two experiences in the past history of God's people. One is very primitive, and reflects tribal wanderings in the desert. God was thought of in terms of the many nature spirits found in mountains, streams and trees. These spirits were unpredictable. If you pleased them they could help you; if you upset them they could make things go horribly wrong. Jacob wrestled with one at Peniel and his hip was put out of joint for life. God could make it rain and drown everyone in a flood, or could cause an earthquake and destroy whole towns. But if you sacrificed enough animals and poured the blood on altars, you might get God to regard you favourably.

The other picture is drawn from more civilised times when the Jewish people were ruled by kings and queens and the great nations around also had kings, queens and emperors. These were usually tyrants. They had the power of life and death over their subjects; they wrapped themselves in majesty and pomp; they sat on thrones, surrounded by admiring courtiers, exercising judgement and leading their soldiers into battle. They could be pleasant like David, famed as a poet and a musician, or they could be nasty like Ahab and Jezebel. The Old Testament God is a king, for the most part a benevolent despot, but a despot all the same. The God of Old Testament religion is thus a God we are afraid of – 'fear of the Lord is the beginning of wisdom' – a God we bow before in awe and reverence, but have to make a real effort to love.

These pictures of God exist in both Hebrew and Christian scriptures. Elijah slaughtered the prophets of Baal in the name of this God in 1 Kings, and Rocky gives Nye and Sapphire a heart attack in the name of the same God in the Acts of the Apostles. God is clothed with majesty as an earthly monarch and sends down judgements on the wicked in the Hebrew Psalms. He does the same in the Book of Revelation in our Christian scriptures.

But in both Hebrew and Christian scriptures there is another picture of God. In Psalm 23, God is a shepherd who cares for his sheep. In John's Gospel Jesus is that same Good Shepherd who gives his life for the sheep. In Hosea, God is a lover, so much in love that he forgives and takes back his wayward partner again and again and again. In Luke's Gospel Jesus portrays God as a parent who welcomes home a delinquent teenager with a party and a dance band. In Isaiah of Babylon there is a god-like figure (a servant who behaves like God, his master) who suffers to redeem others. On the cross Jesus prays, 'Father forgive them; they do not know what they are doing', probably with that picture from Isaiah in his mind. Even in the Book of Revelation where the Lamb receives the worship accorded to an earthly monarch writ large, Jesus stands at the door and knocks.

We have throughout the Bible the choice between Old Testament and New Testament pictures of God. In Samaria, when Jesus refused the request of James and John, he resisted the temptation to revert to the Old Testament picture.

How we relate to God

The word 'covenant' means 'relationship' or 'agreement'. In Old Testament religion people relate to God by means of keeping rules. You do what God wants without question, and what God wants is clearly expressed in a code of law. Moses provided the Ten Commandments in the name of God and he and others provided many other laws besides, some of them helpful and reasonable, others less obviously so. But, whether you like the laws or not, whether you can see any point or not, whether you think the law is cruel or not, you do what you are told, otherwise the covenant is broken and God will no longer protect you. Pious Israelites believed that it was because they had broken God's laws that they had been taken into exile. Paul in his letters from time to time advocated that certain Christians who had gone a bit too far in expressing their new-found freedom should be put out of the fellowship. (Though he could then change his tone and plead for them to be reinstated!)

Jeremiah saw the need for a new covenant that would not depend on the keeping of rules but on an instinctive understanding of what God wanted. In this new covenant, no one would dream of telling anyone else what to do; each would be able to work it out for themselves. At the meal Jesus held with his friends in the Upper Room, Jesus announced that the time of the New Covenant had come. Paul also, for all his inconsistencies, argued that we are brought into a relationship with God not by what we do, but by trust. The relationship is expressed not in terms of slavish obedience, but in loving cooperation.

The Samaritans may have gone easy on the rules according to the Jews, even on the rules of hospitality. But Jesus sought to relate to them on the basis of eating and drinking with them, thereby establishing friendship, and not on the basis of Brownie points. He wanted them to join his community of tax collectors, prostitutes and criminals, saved not by fear of punishments but drawn by love. We have to choose between these two ways of relating to God, by rule keeping or by a friendship based on loving trust.

HOW WE REGARD ONE ANOTHER, ESPECIALLY OUR ENEMIES

The world of the Old Testament is a world of 'goodies' and 'baddies'. There are saints and sinners, there are friends and enemies, there are those who deserve honour and attention and those we may despise. 'The wicked are like the chaff which the wind drives away' (Psalm 1). John the Dipper had the same mindset. 'The chaff he will burn with fire unquenchable' (Matthew 3:12). In the Old Testament, the tribes of Canaan are in the way of the Israelites, so they are therefore God's enemies. So God can be relied upon to help the Israelites to exterminate them, Dalek-fashion. In the Book of Revelation, the enemies of God and God's people are consigned for eternity to a lake of fire and brimstone.

But in the Book of Jonah, God cares for Nineveh, the capital of Assyria, which has conquered much of Israelite territory and taken its people captive. In the Book of Ruth, God's love is revealed in the relationship between a Jew and a Moabite. (The Moabites were traditional enemies of the Jews.) Jesus applied the call of God to love one's neighbour to the story of a Samaritan overcoming his prejudice to help a Jew in his time of need. Stephen prays forgiveness on those who stone him to death, and Paul, who persecutes the Christians, is called to be a front-line Christian activist.

We have to choose between the Old and the New Testaments in our relationship with one another. Do we relate on the basis of a competition in righteousness? On the basis of, 'You come our way and we'll accept you'? 'Since you persist in rejecting the truth we offer, we'll confine you to our mental rubbish bin, confident that God will do the same"?

The God of the Old Testament is a 'jealous' God, and his people are jealous too. The God of the New Testament is a God who loves without end, and his people never give up loving either.

> God is; God is as seen in Jesus; that is our ground for hope. (Bishop David Jenkins)

Chorus

> Turn your eyes upon Jesus;
> Let judgement and anger give place;
> And then those you fear will grow strangely dear
> In the light of his wisdom and grace.

> Turn your eyes upon Jesus;
> Look full in his wonderful face;
> And the world's despair will inspire your prayer
> In the light of his beauty and grace.

4
Who's First in the Queue?

Luke 12:13-15; 18:15-17 and Thought-Provoking
Sayings of Jesus – Gospel of Thomas, sections 72-75

> Someone in the crowd shouted out to Jesus,
> 'Teacher, my brother's done me out of my
> share of the family property. Tell him to put
> it right.' Jesus said, 'I'm not a judge. I'm not
> qualified to decide your case. But I will say
> this, to you and to everybody else: Watch
> that monster "Greed". Quality of life
> doesn't depend on how much money or
> property you have.' (Luke 12:13-15, *Good
> as New*)

> Some people were bringing their children to
> Jesus for him to hold. His friends told them
> to leave Jesus alone. But Jesus asked for
> them to be brought to him. He said, 'Let the
> children come to me; never try to stop them
> – they already belong to God's New World.'
> (Luke 18:15-16, *Good as New*)

Another temptation Jesus faced is illustrated by
comparing two very different stories from Luke's
Gospel. At first glance there seems to be no

connection between them. Yet the behaviour of Jesus in these incidents shows him coming to grips with and overcoming a very common temptation.

The first story concerns someone who requested a favour of Jesus. To understand the request we have to remember that in Israel there was no distinction between religion and the law. Law and religion were one and the legal experts were the religious teachers. It was therefore quite natural to approach someone who had the reputation of being a holy man to settle a legal matter. We know nothing about the man who sought the help of Jesus in this way. Probably he came from the upper crust, for although he had been done out of an inheritance, there was obviously a worthwhile inheritance to be done out of! The vast majority in those days lived on the bread line and would not have prospects of property either to gain or to lose.

The man's request was flattering. It showed that the reputation of Jesus stood high even among the better off. Jesus was not one of the official rabbis, yet this man by-passed the officials because he had greater respect for the fairness and justice of Jesus. Was not such a plea in accordance with the mission of God's chosen representative, the Messiah? The prophets had foretold that the Messiah would be a judge whose justice would exceed all before him.

He will not judge by outward appearances
or decide a case on hearsay; but with justice

> he will judge the poor and defend the
> humble in the land with equity; like a rod
> his verdict will strike the ruthless, and with
> his word he will slay the wicked. He will
> wear the belt of justice, and truth will be his
> girdle. (Isaiah 11:3-5, *REV*)

Had not Solomon, Jesus' royal ancestor, been renowned for his skill and fairness as a judge? (See 1 Kings 3:16-28.) What an excellent opportunity Jesus was being offered to give proof of his Messiah-ship! Jesus brusquely refused the man's invitation to act as arbiter, saying that he had no competence in such matters. Then he lectured the crowd on covetousness, using the man as an example. There is impatience in the voice of Jesus, as if accusing the man of wasting his precious time. The account Thomas gives of this incident bears this out, though in the somewhat sour banter which follows between the man and Jesus, the man responds by accusing the company of Jesus of being wasters (displaying the mind-set of his class?), at the same time indicating his disappointment at not getting what he had come for.

> Then Jesus turned to his followers and said,
> 'I'm not a lawyer, am I? I work out in the
> fields, bringing in the harvest. I'm looking
> for a bumper crop, but I need more help…'
> The man said, 'It seems to me there are

many standing around the bar waiting for a drink, but the tap's run dry!' (Thought-Provoking Sayings of Jesus – Gospel of Thomas, section 73)

Jesus replied with a parable about a party being no fun unless you throw yourself into it, and the story of the seeker of fine pearls. Whether his words had any effect on the man we are not told.

What temptation was Jesus resisting? Possibly there was the chance of a financial reward, something towards the travelling expenses of Jesus and his disciples. That can be ruled out. Jesus could not be influenced by money, though there was at least one member of his circle who could. Jesus also seems to have been particularly immune to flattery. But the opportunity for some good, positive publicity may have interested Jesus. Jesus understood that a good product does not sell without adequate promotion. After all, he was on a promotions tour for God's New World!

The best way to understand what the temptation was about is to have a look at the second story. This story is one of the best known of the Gospel stories. It is appropriate reading on Mother's Day ('Mothering Sunday'), and also when children receive their welcome into the family of the Church, by whatever rite. Many years ago they sang in Sunday School,

When mothers of Salem their children
brought to Jesus,
The stern disciples drove them back and bade them
depart;
But Jesus saw them ere they fled and sweetly smiled
and kindly said:
Suffer the children to come unto me.

It is just as likely that it was fathers who brought the
children to Jesus, since it was the father in that society
who had the responsibility for his children when it
came to religious duties, such as seeking a blessing. Or,
more likely still, it was outcasts who were bringing
their children because they could not get a blessing at
the synagogue, the children of tax collectors and
prostitutes, one-parent families and the like. This time
it was the disciples who were brusque, taking their cue
from their teacher, as they thought. The children may
not have been as well turned out as the children of Mr
X with the legal problem would surely have been.
'What do you mean by pestering the Teacher; don't
you realise he has better things to do?' If Jesus did not
have time to spare for someone from the middle
classes, surely he did not have time for these
dishevelled peasants?'
   This time it was the disciples who were put in their
place and treated to a lecture. We are told that Jesus
was angry, not a very common occurrence, all the
more noteworthy. Mark gives us a fuller account at
this point. Luke maybe has some sympathy with the

awkwardness some Christian disciples feel in the presence of children.

> People were bringing young children for Jesus to hold, but his friends tried to shoo them off. This made Jesus very angry and he said, 'Let the children come to me; never try to stop them. They already belong to God's New World. In fact, anyone who doesn't naturally accept God's New World in the way a child does, has no chance of being part of it.' Then he took the children in his arms, cuddled them and made them laugh.
> (Mark 10:13-16, *Good as New*)

The poor disciples, would they ever get to understand their teacher and his unpredictable behaviour? It looks as if Jesus was having a rest day, or a siesta perhaps. These people were of no significance or influence. Nowadays they would have been invited to make an appointment for a later date. But Jesus gave up his rest period, embraced the little crowd, spent some time with each child, engaging in children's talk and giving each a dose of happiness (blessing).

The temptation that came to Jesus on both these occasions, and at other times, was to attach importance to status and position. Society grades people according to class, wealth, attainments, influence or fame. So do we, however much we may deny it. The media won't allow us to do otherwise. It would be good for ministers to mark how in the case of some callers they insist on an appointment, whereas others are guaranteed a 'Do come in, how nice to see you!' whenever they may chose to call – not close friends, but 'important people'. Few would keep a wealthy subscriber standing at the door to be told the vicar is too busy to see them today.

What made Jesus 'Messiah' was not his ability to take on complex legal cases, but his ability to ignore social distinctions. If he had priorities, it was towards those whom others neglected and despised. But he loved everybody, including Mr X, and dealt with each in the way each needed most. According to Thomas, Mr X was in no way sent packing, only his specific request refused. Jesus afforded him the opportunity for an extended conversation.

Most of us are toads at heart. I confess to having been over the moon when, for the second time, I was invited to be mayor's chaplain in Pontypridd. I especially enjoyed walking in the procession with the band playing! But I know that I should consider it a greater privilege to have visited men in prison in Dartmoor and Pentonville, Cardiff, Swansea and Usk, and in my heart of hearts I hope I do. But the mayor and her husband were important too. Jesus does not want us to pick and choose. Like him we must learn to receive people as they come, and be neither snobbish nor inverted-snobbish. My father, an ace pastor, liked to sit on a park bench or at a bus stop where there was a seat and wait for someone to come and sit by him for a chat. He had some good company that way. It was the way of Jesus.

Above all, we should never look down on children or exclude them from the New World Banquet. According to Jesus, they have the most right to be there. There are no grown-ups in God's New World, no one who has attained sufficient age, learning or status to receive special privileges.

Prayer

Loving God, Jesus advised us to be humble. This is a hard one, even harder perhaps than loving our enemies.

The more we try to be humble the less humble we become. If we think we've succeeded, we've failed completely.

Humility is a spiritual attainment, which, more than any other, relies on your grace and not our own effort.

So we admit we do not possess humility; we are not going to struggle to attain it; we ask you to give it to us as a free gift. Make sure we do not notice the gift when it comes, or we shall lose it.

Amen.

5
Keeping the Peace

'My mission in life is to bring about a
revolution, and I'm longing to see the sparks
fly! I have a painful time ahead of me, and I
can't wait to get it over and done with!
Some of you imagine I'm going to bring
peace to the world just like magic. Quite the
opposite! What I have to say is more likely
to lead to conflict. Families will be split
down the middle, parents and children will
fail to see eye to eye, and newlyweds will fall
out with their in-laws.' (Luke 12:49-53,
Good as New)

One Saturday Jesus was teaching in a place
of worship. A woman came in with a bent
back. She had been unable to stand up
straight for eighteen years. Jesus saw her and
called her to come from the women's gallery
into the central area where the men were
sitting. He said, 'Friend, you're going to
have that back put right today!' Then he put
his arm around her. She straightened up and
sang a song of thanks to God. But the
person in charge of the worship centre was
angry and gave a long lecture to the people.

'There are six days for you to work in. Go to the doctor on one of those days, not on the Rest Day.' Then Jesus said, 'Who are you trying to impress with your self-righteous play-acting? I've seen you Holy Joes taking a donkey or a cow from the stables to the water trough on the Rest Day. This woman is a descendant of Abraham. She's been waiting to be cured for eighteen years. What better day to do it than God's special day?' When Jesus said this, his critics were so ashamed, they didn't know where to look. People started jumping up and down, singing and shouting their thanks to God in appreciation of all that Jesus was doing for them. (Luke 13:10-17, *Good as New*)

Some are born troublemakers. I have always admired those who make trouble in a good cause – young people often, though not always. My heroes and heroines include the Greenham Common Women, those who sit in trees and dig underground tunnels in order to postpone the arrival of a new motorway, anti-hunt demonstrators who turn up in force to spoil the fun, the striking miners, protesting against what they foresaw as the destruction of their communities, and so on. I have always felt guilty that I have never had the courage to throw myself into an activity of this kind. I have been on one CND march – very peaceful – the annual Ash

Wednesday, almost ritual nowadays, procession over Westminster Bridge to the Ministry of Defence to 'deface' its walls with a token smearing of holy ashes. On that occasion, a number of the marchers always volunteer (usually before the march starts) to be arrested and land up in court. Needless to say, I was not one of these volunteers. One year I joined the London Gay Pride March and have a rainbow whistle to prove it. But that is a very ordered and joyful event, planned in full cooperation with the police and authorities and there is never any trouble worth reporting. I stood with one of my sons, holding a lighted candle at a vigil outside Cardiff Castle at the time of the Gulf War. And that is about it! I am a pacifist first by nature and second by conviction, and that is the wrong way round if you are to be deserving of moral credit points. Another way of putting it would be to say that I am a coward by nature and that my convictions are by way of an apology. I have learned that there is nothing inherently sinful about cowardice – it is a tool for survival. But cowardice does not give one a good feeling. As a historian I know that the credal statement 'the blood of the martyrs is the seed of the Church' is at most a half-truth. The martyrs were an inspiration, but the Church would not have survived if the majority of its members had not dived underground.

Where does Jesus come in all this? The authorities certainly looked upon him as disruptive. When

Pilate asked, 'What have you got against this man?' the religious leaders answered, 'We wouldn't have brought him to you unless he were a trouble-maker!' (John 18:29-30). The procession into Jerusalem, though peaceful and integrated with the regular choral processions into Jerusalem at the feasts, had nevertheless a challenging feel about it. Similarly, the cleansing of the Temple which Jesus and his supporters may have made an annual event throughout his ministry. Like the Ash Wednesday March it had come to be expected, but none the less unnerved the establishment. The element of violence was ritual rather than actual, but there was always the danger of things getting out of hand.

Some of the words of Jesus, words we would be grateful to some scholar who could prove he didn't say them, confirm the establishment's view of Jesus. 'My mission in life is to bring about a revolution, and I'm longing to see the sparks fly!' Jesus followed this with words about the inevitability of conflict and families being torn apart (Luke 12:49). Although, with a few exceptions, Jesus managed to avoid situations in which he was involved in physical violence (see Luke 4:28 and John 10:30), the events of Good Friday and the night before were violent in the extreme, and Jesus was a party to them in the sense that he refused to take the opportunity open to him to run away.

So what temptation did Jesus face in respect of public order? Hardly cowardice. Jesus ranks with the bravest of the brave – perhaps the bravest of all time since he always had a canny awareness of the consequences of his actions. Was it, conversely, to use the techniques of the social agitator to draw attention to himself and the just causes of the poor and socially excluded so dear to his heart? No, he caused many an admirer and supporter a deal of frustration by the low profile he adopted in his ministry. In John's Gospel we are told that at one stage, 'Jesus went on a tour of Galilee. He avoided Judea because there were people there who wanted to kill him' (John 7:1-13). His brothers upbraided him for naivety in the techniques of advertising. Spending all his time with Galileans who had no importance on the political stage and no weight socially, was not the way for Jesus to draw attention to himself and his mission! There's a problem here for those who think Jesus was 'without sin' in a Sunday school sense. Jesus told his brothers he was not going to Jerusalem, then did so in secret without their knowledge. A fib! Jesus was not going to be embarrassingly 'outed' by his family, who neither understood his mission nor his methods. (If we are to retain the dogma of the sinlessness of Jesus, which orthodox theologians regard as important, then we should recognise that the sinlessness or (better) moral excellence of Jesus, lay not in a strict adherence to dos and don'ts as per the Old Covenant but in an instinctive discerning of the mind of God as per the New Covenant. Is it always wrong to tell a lie? According to Jesus, No! It is possible to argue on moral grounds, with or without the example of Jesus, that concealing the truth in order to safeguard personal privacy against busybodies is in order, unless criminal activity is in question.)

The temptation for Jesus as he reflected the inevitability of the political and social chaos his words would foment, was neither the temptation to be a coward nor the temptation to be a provoker. It was a temptation best illustrated in the healing of the woman with a bent back.

The story begins with a picture, which could not be more comfortingly conventional. Jesus is going to church! He has been invited to expound the scripture. That means he has the confidence and respect of the leaders of this particular place of worship. They had heard him on previous occasions and he always had something good to say. At the end of the service the scene is anything but quiet and conventional. People are jumping up and down, and there is something of a charismatic revival. But this is after a sticky moment or two.

Jesus had been invited to speak. Why didn't he just fulfil his brief, get some polite words of thanks from the church officers, say goodbye and go home? Because he was aware of the needs of his congregation. He didn't preach and teach in a vacuum. He engaged with his listeners. It's not easy to do this with a large congregation – presumably everybody from the village was there, except a few outcasts. It was a lot to keep your eye on – the leaders in the smart seats up the front, the men of the village, crowded at the back, and the women almost out of sight in the gallery. Despite the glassless windows and an oil lamp here and there, it was gloomy, difficult to distinguish faces and even more difficult to pick out the one with the breaking heart. How easy for Jesus just to let his words do the job for him, to waft to the soul in need. Perhaps such a one would make herself known to him after the service, at the door.

The temptation of Jesus was to allow any considerations whatsoever to get in the way of his prime objective – people in need of being assured of God's love for them. The account says that Jesus called out to a woman. He had to call out – she was a long way away, behind a barrier. We don't know how he managed to spot her, but he did. We don't know how easy it was for her to get to Jesus from where she was sitting, but Jesus called her to step into the main (exclusively male) body of the auditorium. Then he touched her (gasps – some of horror, some of excitement) and he healed her. Then, to crown it all, the woman sang a solo, either at the invitation of Jesus or off her own bat. All this with the mouth of the leader of the congregation wide open in bewilderment and incredulity. Rules and conventions were scattering in the wind. It wasn't just the Sabbath-breaking that might perhaps be a borderline case, open for discussion. A woman had been set free, not only from her deformity, but from the social conventions which enslaved her and her sisters in the gallery. The two aspects of her bondage, physical and social were probably connected. Her bad back may have been caused by the unreasonable burdens she had had to bear for the sake of selfish and unappreciative men. Now here she was, leading both men and women in worship from what was supposed to be the man's privileged position.

There are still a few chapels in Wales where the tradition of the 'After Meeting' continues. At the end of the service, after the uncommitted have left, the meeting may be 'tested' to see if anyone has 'stayed behind', that is, been converted by the preaching. It is also the time for a deacon to thank the preacher for the day, or otherwise as the case may be. Less often nowadays, but not infrequently in days gone by, the preacher was gently or firmly corrected if he had strayed from the path of orthodoxy, or if the deacon simply didn't agree with him. The leader of the synagogue felt it necessary to do his duty in the case of Jesus. The rules had been broken, the bounds of decorum breached. He lectured the people at length, expecting Jesus to conform to convention and fall in line with the call for things to be done decently and in order. Craftily he avoided a direct criticism of Jesus. He threw the blame on the woman and the rest for calling on the doctor unnecessarily outside surgery hours. He thought this stratagem would stave off a comeback from Jesus, whose eye he studiously avoided. No chance. Jesus challenged the hypocrisy of the Sabbath rules, then went to the main point. 'This woman is a descendant of Abraham!' She is not a nobody on account of being a woman, she is not lower than the donkeys taken to be watered at the well. 'She is a full member of God's family, and don't you forget it!' says Jesus. The leader of the synagogue was not an out-and-out humbug, like some of the Pharisees. His was not a case of invincible arrogance. He and his colleagues responded with expressions of shame at the words of Jesus, while the congregation went wild. It might have been different. Jesus might have been escorted roughly out of the synagogue and permanently banned, as had happened in his hometown and elsewhere.

Jesus avoided the temptation to have a debate within himself about whether it would be cowardly to avoid a conflict situation or whether it would be provocative to cause one, by blanking out these considerations completely. All that mattered was responding, according to his understanding of God's mind and nature, to a concrete situation in which human need, both personal and social, was clear and obvious. His followers have not escaped the temptation Jesus overcame on this occasion and throughout his ministry. The women freed by the clear actions of Jesus in his ministry were enslaved again by the Church in the interests of good order and not offending social customs. In many of the first Christian churches, including those where Paul had influence, the woman healed by Jesus would not have been allowed to raise her voice in the presence of the men. The lack of single-mindedness in response to justice and the aspirations of the human spirit has been a persistent strand throughout the history of the Christian Church, as it is still today. Compassion and the correction of social evils have to compete, ever and always, with fear of upsetting the horses. Jesus never went out to provoke, and never avoided provocation. He avoided that two-headed temptation by following the lead of his heart, God's heart.

Prayer

Jesus, we would so like you to supply us with a set of guidelines so we could always do the right thing.

We would like to know when to speak up and when to keep quiet.

We would like to know when to be tactful and when to speak the uncomfortable truth.

We would like to know when we should get involved and when we should mind our own business.

You call some of us to be politically active while others feel they are not so called. Have we got it right in our own particular case?

Are we too timid or too outspoken?

You are not going to give us the answers to our questions.

Accepting you as Leader means learning to do it your way. Playing it by ear, testing the ground, trial and error.

Sensitivity to what is needed in each situation does not come by the book, but by experience.

Kindness and sympathy do not come from some factory. They can only be learned in contact with people.

So help us to be like you.

Help us to get it right more often and wrong less often.

You tell us to be wise as snakes and harmless as pigeons.

Save us from thinking we are experts after we have got it right a few times.

Save us from being discouraged when we have got it wrong.

Inspire us to have another go.

May we have the confidence of knowing that the sum total of our work with you will be your New World, whatever setbacks there may be on the way.

And give us peace in knowing that we are always and forever loved.

Amen.

6
Don't Let them Get you Down

Just then some members of the strict set spoke to Jesus. They said, 'We advise you to get away from this place as quickly as you can. Herod has assassins out to get you.' Jesus said, 'Take that crafty old fox a message from me. "Nothing is going to upset my plans. Today and tomorrow I'm getting on with my work of healing, and by the day after that I'll have finished what I have to do in this town. I'm keeping a tight schedule. I want to get to Jerusalem in time. That's the place God's speakers get killed, not here." ' (Luke 13:31-33, *Good as New*)

I was standing on the platform of Pontypridd station, the longest station platform in Wales, which still today retains some of the original architecture, Egyptianesque in terracotta, though much of it is redundant and sad-looking. The train services have been much reduced and buffet and waiting rooms are now no more. It was 1964 and I had only just moved to Pontypridd with Valerie. We had been married only a couple of months. I cannot tell you now where I was going, or what the errand was. It was a dark night, the weather at its wet worst, but I was feeling good because I had come home to Wales, the land of my birth, to do the job I truly believed God had called me to do. I was accosted by a perfect stranger, a middle-aged man as I recall, who had got off one of the trains and was on his way to the exit. He was in his working clothes. He simply stopped, and without any kind of introduction, said 'You ought not to have come here; they will tear you to pieces.' If I ever saw him again, I didn't recognise him. I was only twenty-five and many people, including the members of my chapel, thought me young and innocent, as in many respects I was – but not in the ways they imagined. They assumed I was new and green to the Christian ministry, whereas I had grown up in a manse and seen the rough and tumble as well as the tears and heartbreak. I was never to encounter anything as bad as what my lovely father had to put up with in one of his churches, neither did I intend to put up with it. My college principal warned the church at my ordination they would be in for a surprise if they tried it on with me, and they should have listened. Neither, as some thought, was I a stranger to Wales and its culture, or to the valleys. My family on both sides were Welsh and most of my relations lived in the Ogwr valley. My parents were part of the diaspora and knew the meaning of the word hiraeth. I had a typical Welsh Mam who could speak Welsh when prevailed upon, and *my* Welsh was more extensive than that of most of my congregation. I had not for many years felt so much at home. So it may be that the sympathy of the stranger – if sympathy it was – was misplaced. There were others who had as much as I to be apprehensive about, one very difficult deacon among them. Some of the other chapels also began to feel threatened when our chapel began to emerge from the hypothermia that had overtaken most of the chapels in those days. However, that eerie encounter on the station platform was not an isolated incident. Not long after, I was walking up Graigwen hill when a neighbour shouted at me from across the road, and I quote in full without apology, 'Don't let the buggers get you down!' The language identified him as a non-chapelgoer. Over the years of my varied ministry in Pontypridd, which has lasted in one form or another for the best part of forty years, I was to encounter a lot of goodwill from such.

Throughout his ministry Jesus received many expressions of sympathy, some of it from outside the ranks of his regular supporters. To some, no doubt, he appeared a pleasant and attractive young man, extraordinarily gifted, but vulnerable in a cruel and heartless world. The Strict Set (the Pharisees) were his enemies. They planned the tactics they would use to get the better of him in debate. But they could not do otherwise than admire his intellect, his sharp wit, and his adherence to his principles, even if those principles differed from theirs. They must also have been impressed by his bravery – or was it foolhardiness – for they could see where his path was leading.

The members of the Strict Set who approached Jesus in one of the villages he was visiting on his final journey to Jerusalem were perhaps trying to unnerve him or may genuinely have been concerned for him. To defeat him in an argument was one thing, to see him fall victim to a gang of Herod's thugs, was another. For his own safety, they thought, this young man would be well advised to go into hiding. There is no need to doubt the sincerity of these people, even if, on taking their advice, they might then accuse Jesus of running scared.

Jesus was not going to lose his nerve. But he might nevertheless review his itinerary. It would indeed be tragic if his planned entry into Jerusalem and challenge to the authorities were to come to nothing as a result of a stab in the back in some grotty little town across the River Jordan. His friend and relative, John the Dipper, had been such a source of strength and inspiration. It was Herod who had brought about his death. Should he give Herod the chance of a double whammy? Should Jesus just ignore good advice from the well-meaning?

The temptation which came to Jesus at this time was the temptation to be moved by the sympathy of those who were not really sympathisers. We all like sympathy; we all respond to it. But we should always ask not only about the motives, but the commitment of the sympathiser. The Pharisees, or some of them, might be saddened at the thought of Jesus suffering or being killed. But they were a long way from joining his mission of love. Those strangers who offered me so much sympathy and goodwill from outside the walls of my chapel never set a foot inside to help me in my task of breaking down the outworn traditions and attitudes which for many years had hindered the progress of the Good News. How much did they really care for me or my work?

Make sure you take your advice from those who are truly with you and not from those who are just giving you the time of day. Soft-soapers will put you off your stroke, even if that is not their intention. Listen to the advice and pay heed to the criticism of those who are firmly on your side.

However, friend, foe or something in between, may all get it wrong. I have no sympathy whatsoever with the careers of the Campbells, father and son, Donald and Malcolm, who both drove speedboats, each time pushing the speed limit ever further, until at last, inevitably, they had an accident and met their death. Lunacy, it seemed to me. I don't understand deeds of physical heroism such as climbing mountains and lone yacht sailing, which carry with them risks to life and limb, and threaten bereavement to loved ones. But there is no stopping such people, nor is near-encounter with death a deterrent against further and even more dangerous exploits. I suppose I don't understand because for me the cause is not great enough. It was different with Jesus. He was out to save the World. But he shares in common with the Campbells and other 'heroes' the experience that personal satisfaction cannot be separated from mission. 'A man has to do what a man has to do.' Jesus was a lover of life. He desired for himself, as well as for everybody, 'Life in all its fullness'. He did not want to die violently, either at the hand of Herod's assassins, or on a Roman cross. But if the only way to achieve his mission was along that route, then there was no choice. His friend Rocky, when he protested, 'Leader, I'm not going to let this happen to you' and the Pharisee sympathisers-for-a-day with their 'watch out for Herod!' were both the voice of the tempter.

I don't understand the Campbells. I wonder if they would have understood me on Pontypridd station platform that day in 1964? The stranger was half-right in his prognostication. I would crack. Six years of struggle and then a breakdown which lasted on-and-off for fourteen years and from which I will never recover completely. Were they right – those who urged me not to go in for the ministry, foreseeing such an eventuality? I don't believe so. I would not want to go through it all again, but if I had to, I would. My task, though I did not realise it at the beginning, was to found a new church in

Pontypridd, which would break new ground in offering an ecumenical and radical expression of the Christian Good News. I had the personal satisfaction of completing my leg of the relay and passing the torch to others who continued the work magnificently. So the stranger was wrong to suggest that I should not have been there. We must beware of equating happiness and fulfilment with the absence of pain and sorrow, as the world tends to do, today as never before. In the words of the writer to the Hebrews, ('The Call to Trust', *Good as New*)

> Since there are so many spectators watching us from the terraces, let's get our tracksuits off… and let's put all our energy into the race we've been entered for. Let's keep our eyes on Jesus, our trainer, who knows the course from experience. He was so looking forward to the thrill of winning the prize, he put up with the pain of the cross and the jeers of the onlookers. Now he has the seat of highest honour in the grandstand, next to God.

Prayer

Loving God, help us to take the rough with the smooth.

Help us to know when we should enjoy everything

that life has to offer, in a carefree, spontaneous, uninhibited way. For that is to follow Jesus.

And help us to know when there is not much we can expect from life apart from trouble, discomfort and anxiety. May we accept what lies ahead with serenity, perseverance and good humour. That too is to follow Jesus.

Above all, help us not to lose our balance. Help us to experience pleasure without being hooked on it; help us to endure hardship without being grumpy.

In bad times, sustain us with memories of good times in the past and anticipation of good times in the future.

In good times, save us from heartlessness towards the sufferings of others. Turn our experiences of joy into experiences of comfort for *them*.

In the name of Jesus, our Leader. Amen.

7

If you Want my Opinion

Some members of the strict set said to Jesus, 'This New World you talk about, when is it going to come?' Jesus said, 'God's New World is not something you can see. It will never be possible to say, "Look, there it is!" God's New World is here already. It's in people's minds and in their relationships.' (Luke 17:20-21, *Good as New*)

Jesus said, 'If the leaders of your community tell you the New World is in the sky, you'll know they've got it wrong. That's where the birds will discover the New World! To say the New World is in the sky is as silly as saying it's under the sea. That's where the fish will discover the New World! In fact, the New World has no precise location. It's to be found inside you and all around you.' (Thought-Provoking Sayings of Jesus, section 3, *Good as New*)

On one occasion someone asked him, 'Sir, am I right in thinking the full life you talk about is only for the privileged few?' Jesus said, 'If you think the door is small, you must work all the harder to get through it. I tell you, the entrance is getting blocked by all the pushing and shoving. Shall I tell you what it's going to be like for narrow-minded people like you? One day the owner of the house will shut the door, and you'll be on the wrong side of it, knocking and shouting, "Sir, please let us in!" The owner will shout back, "Who are you? How did you get here?" Then you'll say, "You remember us. We invited you to lunch and listened to you when you taught in our town." But the owner will say, "What are you doing here? Get off my property, you're trespassing!" You'll be so angry and upset when you see Abraham, Isaac and Jacob and all God's other friends arriving for the New World, because you'll be outside. People will flock from every part of the world to be at the big party to celebrate God's New World. Those thought of as no-hopers will have the best seats, whereas those who think they deserve special status will be lucky to get a seat at all.' (Luke 13:23-30, *Good as New*)

Although there were undoubtedly some members of the strict set who were after Jesus' blood and didn't mind whether it was Herod's thugs or Pilate's soldiers who did the job, others were content to harass Jesus with a constant barrage of questions in the hope of making a fool of him, thereby discrediting him with the public. The records we have show them making fools of themselves, though the genuine enquirer always received an enlightening answer. Those whose motives were less than honourable frequently received a better answer than they sought, though Jesus raised many a laugh at their expense. Jesus was patient and kind to those anxious to learn. Those pitting their wits against his got what they deserved. The late Donald Soper, on his soapbox at Hyde Park Corner, was a good disciple of Jesus in this respect, as in others.

Jesus was a figure of authority, both with the masses and with his critics. 'This chap knows what he is talking about' was the verdict of ordinary people in the crowd. (Mark 1:22). 'Teacher, we know you're sincere and not afraid to speak your mind. You don't worry what position people hold, you just speak God's truth to them as you see it,' was the oily introduction to one of the most tricky questions the God Squad put to Jesus. (Mark 12:14). Yet the words display a grudging respect. Jesus could not be faulted on his knowledge of the scriptures, though he felt free to challenge them or reinterpret them in original ways. He had always thought his position through, anticipated the questions he was likely to receive and was ready with an answer or skilful evasion. The style 'rabbi' they accorded him suggests the possibility he had received some regular rabbinic training and that he was able to address other rabbis at their level, in academic Hebrew. Here was a man constantly asked for his opinion, day after day, hour by hour, by countless numbers of seekers, upper-class and lower-class, educated and illiterate, honest and false. So this human of all humans must have shared the temptation common to all people in authority or with a claim to fame. He would be tempted to think he knew the answer to everything, to be opinionated. Not only did Jesus not know the answer to all questions, he came clean about it.

On one occasion, the strict set asked Jesus, possibly quite innocently, 'This New World you talk about, when is it going to come?' They were giving Jesus the opportunity to rival the famous oracle at Delphi, or to be a first-century Nostradamus. He could stick his neck out and say 'In about twenty years' time,' or he could, like the seers, dress his reply up in colourful and mysterious language, such as, 'When five eagles fly in from the East' or whatever. Some scholars think that Jesus was himself responsible for the belief that his 'second coming' was to be expected in the lifetime of his hearers. It's more likely that the disciples were to blame for this misinformation. The evidence that Jesus refused to make predictions of this kind is impressive. It must have been tempting for him to hazard a guess. But much of the admiration Jesus still commands today among those who would not call themselves Christian or even identify with any religion, lies in the impression that comes through of someone who confined himself to areas where he knew himself to be competent. Contrary to those who expected a dramatic and obvious vindication of his life's mission (as many still do), Jesus invited people to use their senses to explore the developments already taking place, especially in new patterns of thought and ways of relating. Even here Jesus was not prepared to be specific. He encouraged exploration, not armchair travelling.

On another occasion Jesus was asked whether few or many would be 'saved'. Whatever the enquirer meant by that, Jesus did not use the expression in his answer. However the answer is interpreted, it amounts to a refusal to answer. 'Never mind how few or how many, just make sure *you* find the way,' is one way of understanding the reply. But we are learning to discover how much of the teaching of Jesus, as recorded in the Gospels, assumes familiarity with the patterns of thought of his critics. Without first grasping that Jesus was answering the Pharisees by turning their own pet sayings around, we shall miss the point. The 'pigs' before which no pearls are to be thrown are the strict set who referred to the Gentiles as such. Take care, Jesus says, that you do not become the object of your own scorn by rejecting the good things I'm offering you. In reply to the question about 'being saved', Jesus seizes on the Pharisees' view that getting into God's good books is a minority achievement. It's like being

thin enough, having fasted enough, to squeeze
through a very narrow gap in the wall. (They may
even have imagined Jesus, with his healthy appetite,
having difficulty!) If we read the whole passage
(Luke 13:23-30), it becomes clear that Jesus is
attacking narrow-mindedness throughout. This
bigoted little man and his friends will be so upset
when they see the great Roman roads thronged with
people of all races making their way to God's big
party! So it's the broad way we need to keep our
eyes on! Should we stop singing hymns about the
'narrow way'? We certainly should! To return to the
point beyond dispute – Jesus did not supply his
questioner with a precise figure of the final tally of
the 'saved', or even a rough estimate.

I now show my age by admitting that I remember
a programme on the then 'Home Service' called *The
Brains Trust*. It was an intellectual chat show with a
panel of people considered to be 'brainy'. They were
posed a question, but that was just to get them
going. There followed a profound conversation,
which we, the listeners, were privileged to overhear.
Any Questions (still going!) was the lowbrow
version. Most of the questions on *Any Questions*,
and the panel members, are highly political. The
members of *The Brains Trust* never, to my
recollection, condescended to discuss politics. My
least favourite member of *The Brains Trust* was Dr
Bronowski. Although he was an anthropologist of
some note, he had an opinion about everything,

including religion, which he thought was only for the weak-minded. I suspect that some, at least, of the aspiring intellectual classes, got their views on religion from him, thinking that such a clever man could not possibly be wrong. Although only at the Sunday school stage at the time, I had no difficulty in picking holes in his arguments. I knew he was off his pitch and way out of his depth. Ruth Pitter, whose claim to fame was that she was a poet, and on the panel to provide balance, had no difficulty in seeing him off in her very quiet manner. *Any Questions* works on the basis that a carefully mixed panel of MPs, journalists, industrialists, now and then a bishop or rabbi, can put their minds together in heated argument and hammer out the truth for us. The letters to *Any Answers* show they do nothing of the sort. It's good entertainment all the same.

Neither *The Brains Trust* nor *Any Questions* annoys me so much as those chosen representatives of Christianity who somehow manage to get on to the *Today* programme to tell the waiting public 'what the Bible teaches' about homosexuality, euthanasia, women priests or whatever, when those who know their Bibles realise that what they are doing is giving their opinion on the basis of a tiny selection of shaky texts. But, it would seem, no opinion other than theirs can honestly be held. Thus Christianity comes across as something outmoded, intolerant, irrelevant or bizarre. This happens often and must surely have a very negative effect on the progress of the Good News. It's time Christians adopted the humility to say that there are some problems that are so complicated, requiring so much study and reflection, as well as a knowledge of the real world, that it is simply foolish for the Church to rush to an authoritative judgement. This should apply, for example, to questions of genetic research and experimentation. We should not be hurried by critics who accuse us of not knowing our own mind. We should adopt the practice of Jesus who held back from giving authoritative answers when in his wisdom he knew there were none to be had.

At a service to begin the Week of Prayer for Christian Unity in 2002 in my part of the world, it was good to see all the 'regular' denominations represented. The preacher praised Rowan Williams, the Archbishop of Wales at that time, for his stand on the conflict in Afghanistan after the previous September 11th horror in New York. This pleased me, since the Archbishop's views approximated to my own. But the preacher went on to say how much better it would be if we only had *one* leader, like the Archbishop, who would then tell the world on behalf of us all what the Christian view is on all burning issues. No, no, no! One such leader preached the Crusades. September 11th and the problems in Afghanistan and Iraq are the long-term consequence of his authoritative opinion on behalf of the whole Church! What the Church needs is not a unity of opinion but a unity of understanding, sympathy and humility. Christians need, like Jesus, to resist the temptation to be opinionated.

Prayer

God, why are we Christians so desperate to be right?

Can't we understand what every teacher knows, that being wrong is a step towards greater knowledge, if we truly want to learn?

Why are we so keen for others to agree with our understanding of God, our view on the world, our opinions about what is right and wrong?

Can't we understand that we do not have in our possession all the pieces of the jigsaw? Some pieces are held by others. Only when we see where their pieces fit will we be able to see the whole picture.

Why do we feel so insecure when we are challenged? Why are we so determined to control every encounter with another mind?

Can't we understand that God speaks to us in many ways and that we shall miss what God has to say if we only have one channel on our receiver or if our phone cannot take incoming calls?

Why must each of us fashion our own brand of
fundamentalism while condemning the other
available brands?

Can't we realise every window we close is one less
for the Spirit to fly in through?

Why must we annoy others by not really listening to
what they have to say?

Why not let their questions intrigue and excite us
instead of causing our impatience?
Don't we know they are made in your image, just
like us? Their minds are as capable of perceiving
your truth as ours.

Save us from being tiresome, boring, opinionated
cranks!

Amen!

8
The Desert Invades the Garden –
Gethsemane Communion

Jesus left the hotel and took his usual route to Olive
Hill, with his friends close behind him. When he
came to his favourite spot, he said to his friends,
'Ask God to keep you out of trouble tonight.' Then
he went a little way from them, knelt down and
spoke to God. He said, 'Loving God, please don't let
me have to go through with this. But if it's what you
want me to do, I'm ready.' As Jesus said this, he
experienced a great upsurge of strength, and he
knew that God had not left him on his own. But the
pain of grief and anxiety was so intense as he
opened his heart, the sweat fell from him in huge
drops. (Luke 22:39-44, Good as New)

When, in our imagination, we enter the Garden of
Gethsemane, we are treading on 'holy ground'. The
word 'holy' means 'different' or totally other from
what we are capable of experiencing or imagining.
But the Gospel writers all take us there,
notwithstanding. They allow us the tiniest of
glimpses into the severe struggle within the mind of
Jesus, so intense and so acute as to produce physical

agony, seen as drops of sweat like clots of blood falling to the ground. The struggle includes the presence of temptation. There has been nothing like this in the experience of Jesus since that six weeks' sojourn in the desert, only this is much worse. The desert has invaded the garden. The joyful lover of life is now experiencing life's nasty side. The very place that had served so often as a retreat for rest and relaxation, among the olive trees and sweet-smelling flowers and herbs, has become the place of gloom and terror. The 'devil' in the shape of doubt, bewilderment, anxiety and desolation, is in charge of the agenda. Was this falling apart of everything happy, positive and life-affirming really part of the course, or had he taken a wrong turn somewhere? Did he have to drink this cup in order to be the Complete Person he had determined to be? He was frightened by the prospect of suffering and shrank from it, as would anyone in their right mind. He knew it would be very bad. He knew that strength had been given by God to the martyrs of times past. Would he, like them, keep his composure, whatever the pain? Or would this ordeal prove him unfit to be counted among their ranks? His temperament was far removed from that of the gladiators in the arena or the tough regulars in the Roman army. Once they had set themselves to do what they had to do, they got on with it, almost oblivious to the pain. Could someone so different from them display the same kind of fortitude, or would he turn out to be a

wimp? 'Be yourself,' was his advice to others
(Matthew 16:26). Was he really being himself by
opting for such an extreme physical test? He
certainly did not expect it of his friends. He had
suggested they should run for safety (Luke 22:35-
38).

Suing for compensation has become a growth
industry. Anyone who feels they have been hard
done by is encouraged these days to find somebody
to blame and sue. People who suffer as a result of
someone else's carelessness or malice should receive
some token from those who do them wrong, if
possible, though often the amounts of money sought
are ridiculous, the symptom of greed rather than
injury. We seem to be forgetting that we live in a
dangerous world where all sorts of things are likely
to go wrong and that we cannot hope to get a sweet
for every bump we receive. Among those who seek
compensation are those who have made the armed
forces their career and developed illnesses physical
or psychological in the line of duty. We should do
our very best for such people, for they are victims of
a state that continues to glorify war. However,
someone should have warned these innocents that
war is all about giving and receiving injuries. Such
injuries are frequently incapable of being
compensated, not because the money is unavailable,
but because there are some things that money can do
nothing about. Jesus was no innocent. He
understood that life is precarious and that his chosen

career increased greatly the already high chances of danger to life and limb. But was he up to the challenge?

However horrible the contemplation of the physical pain in store for him, there was much more for Jesus to agonise about. There was doubt. How glibly we say that without doubt there is no faith. Perfectly true, but Gethsemane is not about a student writing a theological essay. Here is a man fighting not only for his life, but also for his sanity. Jesus was not cocksure. Jesus is not understood by those who can only cope with him as a golden idol and not as a real person. Yes, there had been moments of revelation and conviction, backed up by the confidence of the friends he trusted. But what if it were all delusion? He taught people not to be arrogant and ambitious. In entertaining the thought that he might be the Messiah, had he himself fallen into the devil's trap? Had he interpreted the scriptures rightly? His way of understanding the Hebrew writings was so different from the other authorities of his day. Was he too way out? If his teaching was so obviously the truth, why were so few of his fellow rabbis convinced? Was he making a fool of himself? Were they laughing behind his back?

A yet more disturbing thought – was his quest for 'life to the full' leading him towards completion in an act of masochism? Some achieve a twisted, ugly excitement through pain. Did he have a martyr complex? Did he wish to draw sympathy to himself and his cause by being a victim? Was he committing suicide? Would God the creator of life be happy at his throwing away his life so carelessly? A stab in the back or a stoning by an enraged crowd, or arrest by the authorities when he was off-guard? That would be true martyrdom – unplanned, unsought! But to hang around like this, waiting for them to come and get him? There was so little time to make sure. Judas was already on his way. He and his friends could just escape in time if they were quick. If the cross were to prove a mistake, it would be the biggest mistake of all time. A wonderful ministry of teaching and healing cut short by an act of terrible madness.

The one thing that was so special about Jesus was his love for humankind. Hitherto his love had been so sure a guide for his line of action. Now it was tugging him both ways. He would be inflicting grief and fear, abandonment and despondency on those he loved, not only his nearest and dearest friends, but on all those whose lives had been changed by him, those he had healed, those he had comforted, those he had partied with. How would delicately balanced people like Maggie and Larry take it? Yes, he was about to make his greatest sacrifice, to crown a life of giving himself for others. But this would only happen if the people he loved committed their greatest sin. Was Jesus to be responsible for creating the scenario that would provoke humankind to offend God's majesty in a way more terrible than ever before? He would be party to their crucifying God's anointed! Should he make it possible for folk to commit so bloody an act, so unpredictable in its consequences? Wouldn't he be to blame for their sin and for their damnation?

Love is a mystery. It seeks another's highest good, but often tumbles over itself in so doing. Love bound Jesus to others. But now he was to cut the cords. He would stand alone, isolated, towering over a world of humankind in self-effacing grandeur, while his loved ones would sink to their lowest depths. One friend would even take his own life. Which way was love pointing? Perhaps this was the cup he wanted to avoid – the poisoned chalice that would cause maximum breakage to his heart of love. He wanted the best for people. The cross would show them at their worst!

For us too, love often involves the same temptation. We are tempted to avoid pain for ourselves and for others. We dodge the issue; we think better of our favourites than they really are; we are afraid of bringing things into the open; we put off vital decisions. This turns the relationship of love we value so much into fantasy. Humanists often set themselves up for disappointment and disillusionment by being over-confident about the ability of human beings to respond to education and good influences.

I have been involved at several points in my ministry is assisting churches of different denominations to forsake their separate buildings and unite together. It is a very Christian exercise, which always tests the basic Christian loyalties of the members. This rarely has anything to do with theology or church government. It has to do with group dynamics and the art of living together. Never has such a uniting (without any doubt what Jesus wishes for his people) happened, in my experience, without an element of tragedy. Mr Jones and Mrs Evans who have been such loyal and faithful members of Bethel for years, have always been so nice to everybody – even to those in the other church when they did not have to go there – reveal a side to their characters discreetly hidden until now. They throw their weight about in a most unhelpful manner; they find all the lame excuses in the book why they should not go along with the proposed merger; finally they take umbrage and go off in a huff. It is bound to be heartbreaking for the minister who has so lovingly cared for them over the years and for the other members of the church who have been their friends for so long. Is it this heartache which makes so many leaders reluctant to go down the unity road? You cannot make an omelette without breaking eggs. But what if those eggs are people?

There had to be a moment in time and history when God and humankind achieved complete honesty with each other. At the cross God's love was shown without question mark. Neither was there any question mark against the sin of humankind. Jesus avoided the temptation to allow his love to paper over the cracks. The true love of God within him took him past the temporary feelings of the moment to bring about love's highest achievement, on the basis of honesty and realism. As in his life he had shown love to the loveless and the unlovely, so now in his death the full benefits of that love were to be channelled to the whole of humankind. God's Love Story, trailed in first-century Palestine, could now be released world-wide, on the big screen.

At this point in its first draft, this chapter came to an end. I thought I had got to the kernel of the temptation in Gethsemane, and buttoned everything up ready for the publisher. But then I attended a very special and unique service for the retirement from the Christian ministry of my very dear friend and companion in the ministry and on life's road, Michael Ball – or as he was then, for one last hour, Revd Dr Michael Ball, minister of Llanishen Baptist Church, Cardiff. There have been ministerial retirement jamborees before, but this was different. It marked Michael's release from the Ministry of Word and Sacrament. In a moving liturgy, in part devised by Michael himself, he made clear his intention never again to preach or preside at the sacrament, nor to conduct funerals or weddings. The theology of what he was doing was skilfully and sensitively outlined by Myra Blyth, the Deputy General Secretary of the Baptist Union. It was explained to a somewhat mystified and sorrowful congregation of many from Michael's previous congregations and old friends, that there is a distinction, which may be confirmed by scripture, between ordination (the call to a particular role in God's drama) which is for a period, and vocation (the pilgrimage of becoming the person God in creating you set you in the direction of becoming) which is for life. Many in that congregation found it difficult to grasp the more than one point being made by Michael with Myra's help. I suspect this was especially true of the other ministers present. They would have understood if there had been any suggestion that Michael had lost his faith, but his faith remains unusually strong. They would have understood and sympathised if there had been evidence of burnout or if a medical practitioner's report had recommended a rest. There was no such evidence to calm their anxieties. This man was giving up his job at retirement age, like most other people.

No mention was made of Tolkien, or of the ring, or the amazing difficulty all who hold power have of giving it up, or of the pathetic and destructive Gollum. But I thought about it in bed that night. I am not a fan of Tolkien, despite reading him right through. He goes on too long (!). But the point he makes, also made by Wagner, and by Lord Acton in his famous dictum 'Power corrupts', is a stern warning to those who happen to wield power, and must include those who wield the strongest power of all, the power entrusted to religious leaders over the souls and minds of others. When you are aware you have gifts of leadership and insight and experience, and when others whose opinion is respected strongly confirm your appraisal of yourself, to say nothing of those less distinguished but proficient in flattery, it is as hard to let go of your position as it is for a dog to let go of a bone. Nearly all the Prime Ministers of our offshore European island in the last century went on too long and thereby spoilt their distinguished careers. Harold Wilson was an exception. I remember being quite upset at his retirement. But he was right. He could so easily and accurately have argued, as the other Prime Ministers did, that he had not yet completed the job, that his country needed him, that he would go one day in the not too distant future, but now was not the right time.

The bitter cup Jesus was called upon to drink, and which he was tempted to set on one side, included all the things I have mentioned – physical and mental suffering, sorrow and trauma to friends, public disgrace for himself and much bigger disgrace for his own people and for the world. But I now see that I must add, to all this, the reluctance to let go. Jesus was the leader of a new religious movement, a movement with an idea that could change the world for the better. He was being asked to bow out as leader and to allow others to take over. What a prospect – Peter, James and John! They couldn't even keep awake while he was praying! The whole bunch were quarrelsome, disunited, lacking in imagination, tradition-bound, self-seeking, faithless and treacherous. They would turn his vision for a new humanity on its head the moment they lost sight of his physical presence. Jesus was only in his thirties, for heaven's sake, why be so hasty or so rash? With a bit more training perhaps, more time under his influence, his disciples might shape up? Maybe others would emerge more suitable to be his successors? Jesus set aside all such considerations and went on his way to the cross, thus removing his physical presence and handing over the work to his unprepared and incompetent staff.

We have no difficulty in seeing Jesus in the garden opting for love instead of power as the means to a brighter future for the world. Our problem is in following his example when it is time, perhaps long overdue, that we relinquished our power. Jesus did not cling on. Why must we?

GETHSEMANE COMMUNION

Leader: Jesus said, 'Can you drink the bitter cup I'm going to drink?' Friends of Jesus said,

All: 'Count on us!'

Leader: They sang a song to God, then made their way to Olive Hill.

Hymn:

Go to dark Gethsemane,
You who face decision's hour;
There you will your Leader see
Torn between his love and power:
Do not shun the sweat and tears;
Share with God your hurt and fears.

Follow to the judgement hall;
See an honest man on trial;
Watch him face accusers, all
Filled with jealousy and bile.
For us Jesus takes the cup –
Drinks the bitter mixture up.

Time to climb the skull-shaped rock,
Scene of many a cry of pain;
Righteous hiss and hoodlums mock
Majesty exposed to shame.
'Father, spare them,' hear him pray,
As you turn your eyes away.

Look, the sun comes out again,
And there's springtime in the air;
Listen to the buntings sing
In the olives here and there.

Even in Gethsemane
Life and Love go dancing, free.
(After James Montgomery, 1771-1854.
Recommended tune 'Toplady')

Leader: Jesus told them, 'All of you will lose your nerve and run off.'

All: *'When the shepherd falls dead,*
The sheep run in dread.'

Leader: They reached a secluded spot near an old olive press.

Sharing: (Plates are passed around containing olives, grapes, dates, figs, spice-mix, etc. All are invited to chose from the selection.)

Leader: Jesus said to his friends, 'Sit here while I talk with God.'

All sing: (Taizé) Stay with me, remain here with me, Watch and pray, watch and pray.

Reader: Jesus took Rocky and Thunder and Lightning a little further. Jesus became distressed and agitated, and told them, 'My heart's breaking. I feel as if I'm being crushed to death. Please stay close to me and keep awake.' Jesus went a bit further on and threw himself on the ground, asking if there was any way of getting out of the horrible things that were about to happen. He said, 'Dear Loving God, you can do anything, so get me out of this!… No, what I want doesn't matter, only what you want.'

Leader: Jesus came back and found the three friends asleep. He said to Rocky, 'Simon, you asleep? Couldn't you mange to keep awake for an hour? Keep your eyes open and ask God to spare you the test. You want to help me, but you haven't got the guts.'

All sing: Stay with me… etc.

Leader: Jesus went away again and talked to God, using the same words as before.

Reader: 'Abba, Abba, Mammy, Daddy – all things are possible to you; take this cup from me. Yet not my will but yours.'

Sharing: (A cup is passed around containing a bitter drink – e.g. salty water, vinegar, neat lemon juice; each drinks or lets the cup pass.)

Leader: Coming back Jesus found them asleep again. They could not keep their eyes open. They were too embarrassed to say anything.

All sing: Stay with me... etc.

Leader: The same thing happened a third time and Jesus said, 'Still asleep and still taking it easy? Enough is enough. The Complete Person is about to be handed over by the traitor to evil people. Up you get! Time to go! Look, here comes the traitor!'

Hymn:
> We sing the praise of him who died,
>> One Friday on a Roman cross;
>> He is our Life – the crucified;
> Compared with him all else is loss.

> The cross! It takes our guilt away,
>> It holds the fainting spirit up;
> It cheers with hope the gloomy day,
>> And sweetens every bitter cup.

> Inscribed upon the cross we see,
>> In shining letters, 'God is love';
> His arms are stretched upon the tree
> To show us friendship from above.

> Those arms! They call us to be brave
> And put our trust in love, not might;
> Their hold is stronger than the grave,
>> They welcome to eternal light.

(Thomas Kelly 1769-1855 Altered)

Pattern Prayer: (Together) Loving God, here and everywhere, help us proclaim your values and bring in your New World. Supply us our day-to-day needs. Forgive us for wounding you, while we forgive those who wound us. Give us courage to meet life's trials and deal with evil's power. We celebrate your New World, full of life and beauty, lasting forever. Amen.

Leader: God cheer you and look after you; God convince you that life is good; God assure you that love is the lasting reality; God satisfy your deepest needs; God give you peace, now and forever.

9
The Last Temptation

When they came to Skull Hill, they fastened
Jesus and the criminals to their crosses. Jesus
was hung between the other two. Then Jesus
spoke to God. He said, 'Loving God, forgive
them. They don't know what they're doing.'
The soldiers threw dice for his clothes. The
ordinary people standing by watched in
silence. But the leaders tried to make fun of
Jesus, shouting things like 'He was good at
helping other people. If he's God's Chosen
Leader, let's see him help himself!' The
soldiers made fun of him too. They paraded
in front of him and offered him some of the
free wine they got for doing the job. They
said, 'If you're the Leader of the Jews,
where's your rescue party?' (Luke 23:33-38,
Good as New)

It had happened. Jesus was on his cross. He had
accepted the cup of suffering and the anguish of
rejection by the humankind he had come to love and
serve. It was his own choice. He had studied the
scriptures and worked out God's way of doing
things. Messiah had to suffer, to be 'despised and
rejected', and it was through suffering that he would

complete his mission. 'It is accomplished' (John19:30, *REB*). As he had decided in the desert, it would not be with armies or politics, not by grandeur and self-display, not by clever tricks, but by the cross. The cross was the climax of a life poured out for others. But the scriptures also said that the Messiah would be vindicated because of his obedience to God's way. People would hide their faces from him, but God would not desert him.

> Yet God took thought for his oppressed servant and healed him who had given himself as a sacrifice for sin. He will enjoy long life and see his children's children...
> (Isaiah 53:10, *REB*)

Well, here was the suffering, here was the cross. Jesus had gone all the way. But where was the expected vindication?

There is a frequent pattern in the Hebrew scriptures. God's servant is in trouble, pushed right to the wall, but at the last moment, in the nick of time, God intervenes and brings deliverance. Jesus had read the book of Daniel. He knew how Daniel was thrown into the Lions' Den, to emerge unharmed. Shadrach, Meshach and Abednego were put into the Fiery Furnace, but God delivered them. This pattern was part of the culture of the Jewish people. If Jesus was to prove himself Messiah, now was the critical moment, the last chance. How the bullies revelled in his perplexity!

> 'He was good at helping other people. If he's God's Chosen Leader, let's see him help himself!'

Even one of his fellow-victims joined in,

> 'You're supposed to be God's Chosen Leader. Let's see you get out of this one! You can give us a helping hand too, while you're at it!' (Luke 23:39, *Good as New*)

These words represent the last temptation. Surely Jesus could save himself if he wanted to? Couldn't he? He could call on legions of angels? Couldn't he? According to Matthew it was an item of faith with him (26:53), but it was never put to the test. Surely the one who had calmed the storm, turned water into wine, fed a multitude on sparse rations, even raised the dead, would have no difficulty in shattering a cross into pieces, would he? We don't know, neither probably did Jesus for certain. We must notice how similar it all is to the reasoning of the tempter in the desert – '... *if* you are God's Chosen...' If Jesus had put God to the test in this way, whatever the result, the outcome would have signalled the failure of everything Jesus had been about in his life and ministry. It would have been a reversion to the Old Testament pattern of vindication and retribution and an abandonment of the New Testament pattern of faith and love.

Perhaps the last temptation consisted of a call to anticipate God's vindication, to induce that vindication to follow the expected and prescribed pattern, the pattern called for by the bullies! We do not have to go along with that cruel, heartless God insisted on as the only 'sound' theology by some fundamentalists. 'The Father's love changes to anger and he turns his back on his sin-bearing son. When he has seen enough blood he changes his mood again.' Not a caricature. I heard it put exactly like this by a young man in his twenties in the chapel in my village in the year 2002! Those God loves God never abandons. But there must be patience, trust and hope, right up to the very end.

The temptation to give in to the 'Let's show them' feeling must have been strong. We know that feeling when the hero in a film is having a bad time of it. All our emotions cry out for him to exert himself to turn the situation round, to neutralise the baddies or bring them to justice. Who could blame Jesus if, just fleetingly perhaps, he contemplated with satisfaction, in his imagination, that look of terror on the faces of the priests and Pharisees, their abuse stopping short in full-flow, were he to come down at them from the cross, while the sky filled with angels. Instead his mind was filled with care for those he loved, watching below or at a distance, for the others crucified with him, and for the soldiers with their unpleasant task. 'Father forgive them…' 'Them' means 'all of them', not only the repentant thief, but the unrepentant thief as well (that spoils a few sermons!), Caiaphas, Pilate, his torturers, the Jewish people as a nation, Rocky, Judas, his own unsympathetic family and anyone else who needed to be forgiven. Jesus stayed on the cross and ended by affirming his faith, 'Loving God, I'm in your hands now.'

This means it's not enough to say that this temptation is about impatience versus patience on the part of Jesus, as if all he had to do was to wait a little longer for God's celebration of triumph! Until Easter Sunday; or if that were not triumphant enough, to the Church's ongoing march, driving all before it; or if that ran into the ground, to a wider movement of the Spirit outside the Church, bringing about 'The Kingdom'; and if that proved disappointing, to a 'second' coming in which, at last, those responsible for the crucifixion would have the smiles wiped off their faces!

> Every eye shall now behold him
> Robed in dreadful majesty;
> Those who set at nought and sold him,
> Pierced and nailed him to the tree,
> Deeply wailing *(sung 3 times)*
> Shall the true Messiah see.

Do we not share with Wesley the desire to

anticipate God's vindication every time we sing hymns of triumph, not only at Easter, but also at Ascensiontide and throughout the rest of the Christian year? When we rush to defend our orthodox faith and practices every time we feel them under threat, from within and without? When we sally forth on 'missions' and 'campaigns' of 'Here we come gathering nuts-in-May' type evangelism? ('Who will we have to pull her away?') When we hunt for devils all over the place, in case the victory at Calvary did not manage to defeat them all? When we deeply resent those who have not had our ecclesiastical tutoring and who read our Bible in a different way, coming to naïve and fascinating conclusions? When we are scared that by letting children read Harry Potter we shall produce a whole generation addicted to witchcraft? What do we have, the mind of Jesus or that of the football supporter, whose team must win sometime if he is to maintain his interest, if not this match then the next? Then there is always Hell, open for business as usual. It seems Jesus did not manage to do anything about that at the first Easter either.

When we look at Easter, as the story is told by the Gospel writers, there is a mystifying lack of triumph. If Jesus had stridden into the High Priest's palace or the Governor's quarters with a great big grin on his face, that would have been something! Instead he went for a walk in the dark with two villagers out in the country. The coming of the Spirit was a bit more exciting, but failed to convince the sceptical. The Church in the Middle Ages did not defeat Islam, despite marching under the banner of the cross, and has been trounced even more miserably in recent times in its battle with secularism. No wonder some Christians pin all their hopes on Armageddon.

It is going to take a much bigger revolution than any that has taken place in the Church's history so far, for Christians to take on board the defeat by Jesus of temptation on the cross. The cross was God's last word about what sort of character God is, and what we can expect of the one and only God in the future. Jesus was completely in tune with the mind of God. So it was not a matter of him meekly going along with the postponement of vindication. With God he rejected the concept of vindication altogether. The pattern of God's revelation in Jesus is the same in his life, his death and his resurrection, and there is no reason to suppose it will ever be any different.

> 'What are you folk from Galilee looking up there for? You've only lost sight of Jesus for a while. He'll come back the way he went, *and he'll still be the same Jesus!*' (Acts 1:11, *Good as New*)

We are the ones who crave vindication; *we* are the ones who want to be proved right; *we* are the ones who want to be members of the winning team!

Those who try to make the Resurrection experience into more of a vindication than Jesus made of it, do so either by insisting that it can be proved historically, as in the clever book *Who Moved the Stone?* or (and these may be surprised to be put in the same category in this way) by arguing for a 'spiritual resurrection' to make it acceptable to the modern mind. Both are trying to make the reality of the resurrection less escapable. Both are trying to prevent the resurrection from appearing to be a damp squib!

God's way, exemplified by Jesus, continues the same. There are no strong-arm tactics, no pressure, no moral blackmail, no inescapable logic, no incontrovertible proof, no forcing people to their knees or obliging them to reach for their handkerchiefs. The father in the story of the Adventurous Son is the God of the death and resurrection of Jesus. The boy comes to his senses of his own accord and the father, far from trying to make him feel small, exerts all his efforts to encourage him to feel big! The God whose name is Love, does not say, 'Look, I'm the winner now!' but 'Look at my cross.' The experience of the resurrection comes to us as it came to Jesus, with the prayer 'Into your hands I commit my spirit.'

At the Cross
(Dramatic Reading)

Narrator: When they came to Skull Hill they fastened Jesus and the criminals to their crosses. Jesus was hung between the other two. Then Jesus spoke to God. He said, 'Loving God, forgive them. They don't know what they're doing.'

Group 1: What are you doing up there, Mr Marvellous? How about showing us a trick? Come off that cross! Or can you only do things with loaves and fishes? God's boy, are you? Ask him to give you a bit of help! Impress us and maybe we'll join your gang!

Group 2: Please Jesus, come down from the cross. We cannot bear to see you suffering there. You are our Leader. We cannot do without you. Give us back our confidence, give us back our hope, give us the courage to face life again. Then we'll follow you to the ends of the earth!

Narrator: One of the convicts who was hanging beside Jesus mouthed abuse at him, saying things like, 'You're supposed to be God's Chosen Leader. Let's see you get yourself out of this one! You can give us a helping hand too while you're at it!' But the other one told him to shut up. He said, 'You should have more respect for God. We're all in the same boat, except that we deserve it because of what we've done. The man you're abusing is innocent.' Then he said, 'Jesus, put in a good word for me when your New World comes.' Jesus said, 'I promise, you and I will keep one another company today, in God's Garden.'

Group 1: What was that he said? Both going to a garden? That's right! You'll both be pushing up daisies soon – after the vultures have had their lunch! Forget the dreams; let's have some action! How about a few angels? Or Elijah? He could put on a good show! You're not even trying! You're pathetic!

Group 2: Oh no! Jesus, please! Don't go off with him and leave us behind! He's no good. Think of his record – never did anything for anybody. Why should he be allowed in your garden? What about us, loyal to the end, still here at the cross, watching and waiting for something to happen? Alright then, you know best. But don't be long. Don't let them think they've got away with it!

Narrator: At about twelve o'clock midday, the sun went in and black clouds settled over the whole country until three in the afternoon.

Group 1: You didn't choose a very good day for it, your high and mightiness. Dreadful weather for the time of year. It's going to rain any minute – better be moving along!

Group 2: So that's your answer God – darkness. No sign of light, no promise of hope. If that's your way for us, help us to follow it.

Narrator: Then Jesus let out a big cry and said, 'Loving God, I'm in your hands now.'

10
Conclusion –
Farewell to Temptation

> So don't be too sure of yourself, or you'll
> fall flat on your face. There's nothing you're
> going through every one of us doesn't have
> to go through at some time or another. God
> is reliable and won't let you get into any
> trouble you can't cope with. God will also
> give you any extra toughening up you need
> and show you the way out of your
> difficulties. (1st Letter to Corinth 10:12-13,
> *Good as New*)

I have always had a bit of trouble with the above text from Paul's first letter to Corinth, which may be translated in many ways, but whichever way, still presents problems for me. On the wall of my study, where it can be seen at all times, is a framed message entitled 'Morning Prayer'. It was given to me by a very dear friend when I was going through a period of much anxiety and stress, including having to look after a demanding and threatening person, with the ever-present possibility of violence.

LORD
Help me
To remember
That nothing is going
To happen to me today
That you and I together
Can't handle

Soon after I had put this on my wall, another of my friends spotted it. Neither an intellectual nor the least bit theological in the conventional sense, his response was swift and curt. 'That's SHALLOW,' he said. I had to agree with him. But it was not just a matter of agreeing with him. It was a matter of bowing to his greater experience. I have always found the words (a passable paraphrase of Paul's text) to work for *me*. They are still on my wall, and not only as a reminder of the friend who made me the gift. But they did not work for my other friend, and that's because he has seen some aspects of life first hand, which I have only seen as from a comfortable seat in the theatre. I am fully prepared to believe that for some who read Paul's letter in Corinth, the apostle's words were the 'Word of the Lord' to them. The words sustained them as they faced, went through, and came out of the time of trial. But I would not be surprised to learn that there were others whose reaction was 'And what does *he* know about it?' Paul suffered much. He tells us all about it, at great length and in great detail. He had learnt the secret of contentment, in whatever situation or state. He received 'grace' to put up with his 'thorn in the flesh'. But what did he know about the life of a slave having to cope with a cruel and abusive master, day after day, year in year out, with no prospect of the promised 'escape'? (2 Corinthians 11:23-30; 12:8-9)

In line with Luther's acid test of submitting every scripture to the judgement of the 'Word of God' (= Jesus), it is difficult to imagine Paul's words coming from the lips of his Leader. Jesus counselled people not to be anxious, to trust and live one day at a time – always good advice, despite the difficulty of putting it into practice. Like all the advice of Jesus, we reap a benefit if we do no more than set ourselves in the right direction. But Jesus promised no emergency exit from situations. There was no escape route as he faced the cross. The only way out was to go through with it, with the chance, no more, of coming out somehow on the other side. Even then he would not emerge unscathed. He would have wounds.

I have heard preachers on Good Friday go to great lengths to explain why the sufferings of Jesus were greater than those of anyone else who ever lived, before or afterwards. For some reason it is important to them that suffering be the hallmark of the life of Jesus here on earth. Even if there are more cruel and long-lasting deaths than crucifixion, they tell their congregations, the suffering of Jesus was also mental and spiritual, his grief and anxiety for the souls of sinful men and women such that he never knew a moment's respite. We have no way of knowing or assessing the suffering of anyone, or assessing their capacity to suffer, an important factor in the equation. But patently, the suffering of Jesus, exceedingly intense in every way, was concentrated very much in his last few days, in particular from the time in the Upper Room to his dying moments. That is not to say that there was not suffering at other periods of his life, the self-imposed discipline of the desert included. But, by and large, Jesus consciously lived a life intended as a sign of the Kingdom, a celebration of the coming of God's New World. His purpose was to call others to join him in this round of celebration, and in so doing he lifted them in company with himself above the anxieties, the drudgeries and the horrors of the first century. It is a negation of the Good News to insist that Jesus was all suffering, and that although we can never suffer as much as he did, we must do our best to do so. That is not Good News but Bad News. A degree of suffering is inevitable for everyone. It is part of life. Martyrdom is inescapable sometimes. But the idea that we should court suffering deliberately is sick. Why did Jesus spend so much of his energies healing people? The projection of a suffering-orientated religion must surely be one of the reasons why so many do not wish to get mixed up with the Church. Most people do not seek pain. Why should they? It has taken two thousand years for a portrait of Jesus to appear, not only smiling, but in the middle of a great belly laugh. I'm told by a colleague in the USA that this first appeared in an edition of Playboy! I saw it first in his church study in Angola, New York State. There are several versions of the picture now, but most Christians have yet to come across it, and the initial reaction is always surprise or shock. Why has it taken so long? What has the Christian Church done to Jesus?

It is time for the Church to bid farewell to its suffering complex. It should also bid farewell to its temptation complex. Part of the problem is language. We persist, as does this volume for sales purposes, in talking about the temptations of Jesus. The majority of Christians when they recite the Lord's Prayer (a mistake to recite it – not at all what Jesus intended!), still use the Cranmer version, 'Lead us not into temptation.' The Church's persistence in hanging on to misleading translations when it has been provided with more accurate ones is puzzling. The newer translations all say something like 'Do not bring us to the test', and that is what the Greek word *peirasmos* means (test, trial, experiment). We persist, by the use of the word 'temptation' in picturing something like an alcoholic walking into a pub, or a smoker who has vowed to give up, deciding to have 'just one last cigarette', or someone who fancies the wife of the neighbour next door booking into the same work-out session with her in the unisex gym. This is not the sort of thing Jesus was about in the desert. His experience was closer to what we experience when we face a critical examination, one that will determine the course of our lives from that point on. We have put ourselves through a period of study or training and now we shall find out whether or not we have made the grade. Even closer is the picture of an experimental think tank where a variety of minds produce a flotilla of ideas, which are then tested to discover which of them holds water. The object of the forty days was clearly not to resist eating or sleeping or sex, though these things were likely a feature of the experience, but for Jesus to put down some positive markers for his career as God's spokesperson.

Enter the devil. The accounts we have picture Jesus in conversation or dialogue with another. This other puts up ideas, which Jesus rejects. His form is not described. It is the meeting of minds that is significant, not a physical manifestation. Why do people get so excited about, and insistent on, the idea of the devil as someone embodied? Does the source of the ideas Jesus spent time thinking about really matter? When Jesus called Rocky 'Satan', he did not mean that his friend had been taken over by a malign force, as sometimes happens in Star Trek. Jesus was responding to Rocky's idea that the Messiah could avoid suffering. The idea was one of the options that came up during the colloquium Jesus had arranged at Caesarea Philippi with Rocky and the others. They were his think tank, his *peirasmos*, his means of testing his lines of thought (Mark 8:28-32). Jesus valued a thorough airing of the options to help him formulate his plan of action. We cannot know whether Jesus had company in the desert from time to time, spiritual counsellors, sought or otherwise. Thoughtful readers of the Bible have often wondered how the Gospel writers got hold of the details of the temptations. The desert was where many of the religious gurus of the time hung out. Jesus may have used one or more of them as a sounding board. What matters is that, in his mind, or in dialogue with others, in solitude or company, Jesus gave himself the time and space in which ideas could compete and possibilities be weighed.

We are sold on the idea that the devil, or 'Satan', is an utterly evil bloke, despite, like everybody and everything else, being dependent on God for his existence. In the time of Jesus it was the overall impression. Satan was held responsible for all types of illness, not just disturbances of the mind. Surprising then that Jesus allowed Satan to keep him company for so long and to put his point of view so cogently. At the end of the period Jesus did not dismiss him. He quietly bowed out. We can only understand this civilised encounter between Jesus and Satan if we allow ourselves to take on board an alternative strand of Hebrew thought which ascribed to the devil a different role from that of evil-doer. In the Book of Job, Satan is a member of God's permanent staff with free access to the boss. His role is to act as a one-person think tank, subjecting everything to rigorous scrutiny. In that ancient drama, probably intended for the stage, Satan questions the sincerity of Job's loyalty to God and God allows Satan to inflict on Job a series of unpleasant tests in order to settle the matter. Satan is not therefore someone to be welcomed by human beings with glee, especially not by those striving towards godliness. He asks too many awkward questions! The encounter between Jesus and Satan in the desert has more of the book of Job feel about it than, say, the encounter between Jesus and the devil responsible for the plight of the man from Kursa, where Jesus got the devil running fast.

We have also traditionally interpreted the story of the Garden of Eden in Genesis 2 on the lines of 'Satan the bad influence', despite the fact that the 'tempter' or 'tester of ideas' in the story is not there identified as Satan. He is a snake, a sentient being belonging to this world, like the man and woman. We are convinced that it was a totally bad thing for Adam and Eve to eat the 'forbidden fruit'.

I started to understand the story when I became a parent and realised that no intelligent parent would put an object highly desirable to their small child in the middle of the room and then forbid the child to touch it. The story is about humankind growing up, losing childish innocence and gaining knowledge in return. It is the story of an initiative test. The two pursue their destiny to become like God, since it is in the image of God they have been made. By jumping the gun they demonstrate a lively impatience to get on with it.

What part does the snake play in the story? Tempter? Yes, if you want to see it like that – a dire warning to make you wary of life, forever on your guard, forever inhibited and uptight. There is no denying that the story may be more simply interpreted that way. But if the story is linked with Job's light on what is happening between Jesus and Satan in the desert, then the snake is a welcome third voice in a debate which enables the first pair to stop mooching around in a garden and come to their first adult decision.

So Christians would do well to drop their obsession with temptation, even in Lent. It rides in tandem with a morbid fascination with suffering and a gloomy outlook on life. This real 'devil', in the form of distraction from the main plot, causes us much unnecessary angst and waste of energy. We should learn from the testing experiences of Jesus. Each consisted of an examination of ideas, followed swiftly by positive action. Should Jesus be a hermit or a *bon viveur*? Options considered and decided-upon in six weeks! Should he have a fixed centre or a roving ministry? Decision made one early morning! Which should he be – trouble maker, trouble-avoider or compassionate helper? Decision made instinctively, on the spot! Cross or no cross? The hardest test of all, draining to the last drop every ounce of emotional and mental energy. But the choice was finalised in a matter of hours. No pussyfooting then! Jesus never allowed 'temptation' to be a time waster, except perhaps in the wilderness, an exercise he significantly did not repeat or recommend to his followers.

I was impressed and heartened on learning that the Bishop of Wolverhampton and his wife, for their Lenten discipline in 2002, were going to try to live on the minimum wage. They 'took up' living on a shoestring. I gathered from the TV programme in which they were featured that this was not a negative token self-denial as in giving up chocolates. They put themselves through a positive learning experience, finding out what it is possible to do and what it isn't possible to do with very little money. I wonder what their consequent Jesus-decision turned out to be? If this sort of 'experiment' (*peirasmos*) is to mean more than the acceptance of temporary restrictions coupled with learning how to beat the supermarkets, then it must continue on to a decision either to adopt the principle of the Life-Style Movement – 'Live simply, that all may simply live', or to a decision that this is not the particular route God is calling you to take or to the third option (also recommended by the Life-Style Movement) the 'FIRST STEP'. This is as much a firm option as the other two but based on a realistic assessment of personal capacity and circumstances, thus avoiding setting oneself up for trial and failure followed by guilt. So often the Christian falls in between the options to perpetuate a temptation-orientated lifestyle. This consists of an unmerry-go-round of try/temptation/fail/guilt/ start again/try/temptation/fail/guilt/start again... ad infinitum. What I am about to say will doubtless be regarded as heresy and dangerous, but having had a limited experience of befriending (not treating or reforming) people with various addictions, I have sometimes come to the view that the addiction is unlikely to come to an end in this life. Putting great thrusts of energy into fighting it can be a soul-destroying line of action, for addict and carer alike. There is an alternative way, I believe (by no means easy or straightforward), and that is to assist the friend to live positively and joyfully, despite the addiction. In one case, I actually saw, to my great surprise, an addiction fade away, but I'm sure this is a very unusual outcome. However, I would say to the rest of us who manage to keep our little 'sins' rather more effectively hidden behind our net curtains, that it's time to throw away the fight with temptation as the key to spiritual improvement and to replace it with a policy of radical decision-making in the light of God in Jesus. We need to abandon the guilt syndrome for which there is absolutely no encouragement in the life and teaching of Jesus whatsoever, and have a go at 'taking up' in place of 'giving up'.

Prayer

JESUS
Help me
To remember
That some things can happen
That overwhelm us utterly.
It happened to you.

Appendix

The Good as New version of the early Christian scriptures – an Introduction

Despite the fact that my shelves, and yours probably, are sagging beneath the weight of all the translations of the scriptures that have appeared in the past forty years or so, we still await a version which strikes as a genuinely contemporary version. Life and language move so quickly that it is a matter of running to stay on the same spot, and translators of the scriptures are characterised by care and caution rather than by the need to keep pace. Move on we must, however, if we believe the scriptures have abiding value for every age and culture as a unique record of humankind's adventure with God.

Two things need to be done. In the first place scholars must continue to study the original languages and explore the cultural situations they expressed. This work has been done very well in the past hundred years and there are commentaries full of sound scholastic argument for the probable meaning or meanings of every word of the received texts. Rarely, however, is there total agreement on the precise meaning of any particular passage, only a study of the options. The choice means that the translator can never avoid bias of a sort. An attempt at word-for-word translation of the Greek or Hebrew, even if possible, would not produce clarity but mystery and ambiguity. In order to clarify, the translator must opt, and this accounts for quite conflicting meanings in differing translations, which nevertheless claim to be true translations rather than paraphrases. Did Jesus say to Simon Peter, 'Do you love me more than all else?' (*NEB*) or 'more than these others?' (*REV*)? Both are possible, but which you choose will strongly affect the total meaning of the incident recorded. It is of no help to take the line of the *NIV*, which translates 'more than these'. This allows us to make up our own minds but is of itself meaningless since we are given no clue as to the 'these' referred to. Too much of this kind of ambiguity will confuse or bore especially the first time reader who is seeking meaning not a puzzle. The common distinction made between a translation and a paraphrase is thus a false one. What usually passes for a paraphrase rather than a translation indicates the degree of venturesomeness in elucidating the meaning. This is what most readers want unless they are scholars, in which case they should be directed to the original languages. We need to warn people that no translation or paraphrase is any more than somebody's intelligent, scholarly, inspired, and, one hopes, honest guess. For those who prefer certainty to faith this is a hard pill to swallow. We should always advise the devotee to have at hand at least two translations in order to preserve choice in the matter of interpretation. The work of scholarship must go on in order to check avoidable inaccuracies and to open up the field of options.

The second thing needed is a combination of 'human skills'. The scriptures were written by real people for real people. We must assume a common humanity between the first writers and readers and ourselves, otherwise we may as well give up from the start. Nobody will communicate anything to anybody. However, within our common humanity people differ. Some people are held to be more 'religious'. Others are thought to be more down-to-earth. Some revel in wandering through the forests of scholarship and doctrinal dispute, others want to get to the point, otherwise they are not interested. The problem is that those who translate the scriptures have always been religious and scholarly and heavily committed in the matter of doctrine. To such people communicating with the rough and ready is difficult and for many of them it does not occur that they need to try. They translate in the language of an academic elite and assume that this is the language that ought to be spoken by everybody else. I remember asking J. B. Phillips in a seminar, what was the essential difference between the language of his translation and the language of the *New English Bible*, which had just appeared. He replied, 'I read the *Daily Mirror*, the translators of the *New English Bible* read *The Times*.' J. B. Phillips produced single-handed the best translation of the twentieth century simply because, at the time, it came nearer than anything else available to the language of the majority of ordinary people. It was thus downgraded in some quarters as a paraphrase, and indeed J. B. Phillips humbly claimed no more for it. Such a view suggested that the other translations were not paraphrases. But who translates more effectively – the one who translates in the language of an enclosed circle or the one who translates in a language understood by everybody?

According to the record of the Gospels, the genius of Jesus lay in his ability to put into language that could be grasped by ordinary folk things that the scribes obscured by their sophistication or pedantry. 'He spoke as one having authority, and not as the scribes.' The trouble is that Jesus' words and the words of his followers have been translated for us over and over again by those very scribes and Pharisees. 'He spoke as one having authority' is, ironically, a good example of a scribe-type translation. What someone in the crowds who heard Jesus for the first time would have said would have been something like, 'That chap knows what he's talking about!' The question of authority is a scribal question ('By what authority do you do these things?'). Jesus was in the business of making God intelligible and lovable to ordinary people. So what is required to turn our scholarly paraphrases into lively translations is the spirit of the founder, the feeling for what makes contact with Ms or Mr Average – imagination and more imagination, based on a common and sympathetic humanity. Imagination is essential for translating and interpreting the scriptures. If you use your imagination you may get it wrong. If you don't use your imagination you are bound to get it wrong!

The *Good as New* version of the early Christian scriptures seeks to be an 'inclusive translation' and this means, in the first place, of those who are neither Pharisees nor Scribes. Ordinary people, even those with university degrees, rarely use correct grammar when they speak. The Gospel-writers used the simplest, most straightforward Greek. It is therefore bad translation to put the Gospels into sophisticated English. We avoid descriptions such as 'Pharisee', which will require the novice to go to a Bible reference book for an explanation. Instead we seek descriptions which are immediate and require no explanation, such as 'one of the strict set'. Some words which started off as common, homely words in the original Greek have been allowed to become formal ecclesiastical terms by not being translated but left in Greek. Thus 'baptise' for the Greek indicated 'dip', but to us it has become exclusively the word for a religious rite, losing its common meaning on the way. When Jesus called Simon 'Peter' it indicated something like our 'Rocky'. Previous translators simply fail to translate and Peter becomes a surname instead of an affectionate nickname. When we see a dove in the street we call it a pigeon! Numerous are the lay folk who when asked to read 'the lesson' say, 'Please don't give me a reading with lots of big words.' Foreign personal names and names of places can be a block to instant comprehension. We have tried in the translations to produce shorter and more familiar names, either by the common practice of shortening, e.g. Nick for Nicodemus, or by choosing a name which reflects the meaning of the Greek or Hebrew name, e.g. Ray for Apollos (the sun god). (The first Christians shortened names in the same way, e.g. Priscilla into Prisca, our 'Cilla'.) We have also translated some biblical place names – Dategrove for Bethany, Fishtown for Bethsaida, etc. thus restoring the meaning they would have had for contemporaries.

More controversial is our principle of 'cultural translation'. We translate 'demon possession' as 'mental illness', which is what the instances in the Gospels would be called by most people nowadays. We can still relate to these stories provided we understand that the purpose of their telling is to illustrate the healing abilities of Jesus rather than to assert the existence of demons.

As the translation has progressed we have also become aware of the need for 'contextual translation'. The Greek can never be translated word for word. Neither should it be translated sentence by sentence or even in some instances paragraph by paragraph. Sometimes the scripture writers developed what they wished to say over longer sections. For example, the words of Jesus about the 'narrow way' have been taken in isolation to mean that the narrow way is the recommendation of Jesus for us. However, Matthew puts the saying in a context that begins with a warning about not judging others and the narrow-mindedness of those who go about looking for specks of dust in other people's eyes (Matthew 7). Looked at in context, the narrow/broad way picture is a favourite picture of the Pharisees which Jesus quotes in order to refute it. We should no more go searching for the narrow way than we should go around looking for specks of dust. Similarly, Paul appears to advocate celibacy by saying as in the *KJV* 'touch not a woman' (1 Cor. 7). A reading of what he goes on to say shows he cannot be advocating any such thing, for he actually tells people not to go without sex for too long. Paul is quoting someone else's opinion in order to contradict it.

'Inclusive' also refers to the inclusion of the feminine experience. The custom of using male language to indicate everybody is no longer regarded as a valid way of translating into our culture. Sometimes it is argued that the culture in which the scriptures were written was male-dominated and that this should be reflected in translation. We are among those who would reply that the ministry of Jesus included a revolt against bad aspects of his culture. His radical inclusion of women among his disciples has been obscured by successive generations of male domination in the Church and the translation of the scriptures since the earliest days has reflected this bias.

We seek to include the experience of the feminine in our understanding of God. That aspect of God theologically understood as the 'First Person' receives no sexual bias at all. 'Father' is translated as 'The Loving God'. The 'Second Person', Jesus, is male, and although maleness is part of his humanity, it is secondary to it. So titles of Jesus lose their exclusive masculine sense. The cryptic term 'Son of Man' becomes 'The Complete Person'. 'Son of God' is translated 'God's Likeness'. 'The Third Person' is regarded as feminine. The Hebrew word for 'spirit' (*ruach*) is feminine. The pigeon, the symbol of the Spirit at the dipping of Jesus is also feminine in Greek (*peristera*). It may be argued that feminine, masculine and neuter categorisation of nouns in a language do not necessarily denote anything other than a kind of convenience. To classify a pen as feminine means nothing in particular. However, when a word like 'spirit', carrying with it the idea of personality and creativity, is classified alongside other words that are also words for persons, such as woman and mother, it is reasonable to suppose that the choice of classification is significant in terms of sexual understanding.

Other radical departures reflect the need to demythologise in order to translate adequately into our own culture. 'Kingdom of God' thus becomes 'God's New World', 'Eternal Life' – 'Life to the full', 'Salvation' – 'Healing' or 'Completeness', 'Heaven' – 'The world beyond time and space' and so on.

ONE was largely responsible for introducing the concept of inclusive language to these islands in its pamphlet *Bad Language in Church* (1981) amidst some scorn. Our position is now accepted by all but the most change-resistant. We hope the *Good as New* translation will prove a fitting outcome of that first stand.

It is important to realise that the *Good as New* translation is unique as a community translation in which all interested Christians, not only members of ONE, have been invited to take part, whether assisting in first drafting, amending, revising the language, offering helpful suggestions or simply pointing out howlers. The project was the brainchild of Michael (Meic) Phillips who also provided the first draft of James, and it was he who encouraged me to set aside other tasks in order to undertake the bulk of the work. I joyfully acknowledge the debt I owe to those, too numerous to mention, whose contributions have provided some of the most inspired and sparkling touches to the translation or who have painstakingly revised the text. Its appearance as a single publication is on the way.

John Henson

ABOUT THE AUTHOR

John Henson is a native of Cardiff and a son of the manse. He graduated in history and theology at the universities of Southampton and Oxford (Regent's Park) respectively and was ordained to the Baptist ministry at Carmel Baptist Church, Pontypridd in 1964. He was responsible for the formation of Pontypridd United Church, a union between his own church and the United Reformed Church, in 1969, and has since given assistance to other churches seeking to make similar unions at the local level. He taught history in Cardiff High School from 1970 to 1973 and then resumed ministry at Glyncoch, Pontypridd in cooperation with the Anglican communion. Since 1980 he has been largely freelance, acting as pastoral befriender to people in minority groups while continuing to assist in the conduct of worship in the churches. He has served as the Chairperson of ONE and also as editor of the ONE folder. He is currently coordinator of the Good as New version of the early Christian Scriptures (a community translation), together with Michael Phillips. His interests include left-wing politics, penal reform, peace, the quest for truly contemporary and inclusive worship and gender issues. He has lectured on faith and gender in Strasbourg and Oslo at the invitation of the European Union and the World Student Christian Federation. He continues to teach the piano. He is happily married to Valerie, his partner for nearly forty years. They have three adult children: Gareth, Iestyn and Rhoda, and to date seven grandchildren – Aidan, Bleddyn, Carys, Gwenllian, Dyfrig, Iona and Isobel. This is the fourth of John Henson's books; the others are Other Communions of Jesus, The Bad Acts of the Apostles and Gems Reset and Buttons Polished (volume 1).